Mastodons to Mississippians

TL &H | TRUTHS, LIES, AND HISTORIES OF NASHVILLE

TRUTHS, LIES, AND HISTORIES OF NASHVILLE
Betsy T. Phillips, *series editor*

As a lead-up to Nashville's 250th anniversary in 2029, Vanderbilt University Press is publishing an ambitious new series consisting of twenty-five small volumes designed to bridge the gap between what scholars and experts know about the city and what the public thinks it knows. These are the stories that have never been told, the truths behind the oft-told tales, the things that keep us in love with the city, and the parts of the past that have broken our hearts, with a priority on traditionally underrepresented perspectives and untold stories.

MASTODONS

TO

MISSISSIPPIANS

ADVENTURES

IN

NASHVILLE'S
DEEP PAST

AARON DETER-WOLF
& TANYA M. PERES

VANDERBILT UNIVERSITY PRESS
Nashville, Tennessee

Library of Congress Cataloging-in-Publication Data
Names: Deter-Wolf, Aaron, 1976– author. | Peres, Tanya M., author.
Title: Mastodons to Mississippians : adventures in Nashville's deep past /
  Aaron Deter-Wolf and Tanya M. Peres.
Description: Nashville : Vanderbilt University Press, [2021] | Includes
  bibliographical references.
Identifiers: LCCN 2021009786 (print) | LCCN 2021009787 (ebook) | ISBN
  9780826502155 (paperback) | ISBN 9780826502162 (epub) | ISBN
  9780826502179 (pdf)
Subjects: LCSH: Nashville (Tenn.)—Antiquities. | Mississippian
  culture—Tennessee—Nashville. | Mounds—Tennessee—Nashville. | Indians
  of North America—Tennessee—Nashville—Antiquities. |
  Paleo-Indians—Tennessee—Nashville. |
  Archaeology—Tennessee—Nashville. | Paleontology—Tennessee—Nashville.
Classification: LCC E99.M6815 D48 2021 (print) | LCC E99.M6815 (ebook) |
  DDC 976.8/5501—dc23
LC record available at https://lccn.loc.gov/2021009786
LC ebook record available at https://lccn.loc.gov/2021009787

CONTENTS

ILLUSTRATIONS

ACKNOWLEDGMENTS

We thank our many colleagues and the members of the Nashville community who spoke with us about their research, experiences, and memories of Nashville archaeology. Alan Brown, Brian Butler, John Broster, Larisa DeSantis, John Dowd, Nick Fielder, Shannon Hodge, Don Hubbs, David Sims, Kevin Smith, Jesse Tune, David Wilson, Ron Zurawski, and others graciously shared their expertise during uncertain times. Mauricio Antón, David Dye, Lacey Fleming, Les Leverett, Noël Lorson, Robert Sharp, Debbie Shaw, and the staff of the Tennessee State Museum all contributed or assisted with images. We also wish to thank Tennessee state archaeologist (now retired) Mike Moore, for over a decade of support, encouragement, and steady guidance.

We offer acknowledgment to the Native American communities and individuals who for millennia have made their homes in the Cumberland River valley of Middle Tennessee, and whose ancestral sites have been displaced by historical and modern development. Through careful and considerate examination of the archaeological record we hope to increase understanding and respect for these cultures, their accomplishments, and their legacies.

CHAPTER I

Making Sense of Nashville's Deep Past

In 1845 workers digging a well on William Shumate's farm, located seven miles south of Franklin, uncovered a giant skeleton. Around fifty feet below the surface the well shaft encountered a fissure in the limestone bedrock, at the base of which lay a collection of massive bones belonging to an American mastodon. This was not the first mastodon discovery in America, or even in Tennessee. By that time, remains of *Mammut americanum,* an extinct species of ice age elephant, had been recovered from various locations throughout the eastern United States for more than a century. Those skeletons were enthusiastically reported on in newspapers and historical texts, and displayed with great fanfare in natural history museums of the era.[1] In his 1823 work *The Natural and Aboriginal History of Tennessee,* Judge John Haywood, also known as the "Father of Tennessee History," reported discoveries of at least five fossilized elephants in Tennessee.[2] By 1845 and the discovery on Shumate's farm, the total number had climbed to nearly twenty.[3]

Like many fossil skeletons of the era, the Shumate Mastodon was displayed for the public's viewing pleasure. There was, however, a twist: mounted upright on two legs and improved by the addition of wooden pieces to replace missing portions of the skull and pelvis,

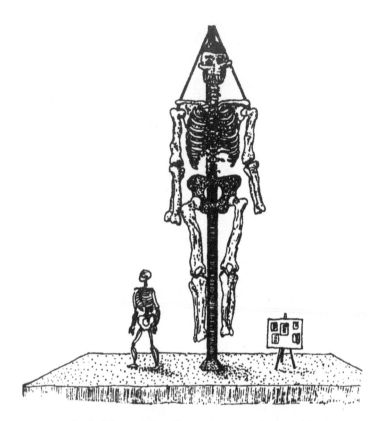

FIGURE I.I. Sketch of Shumate's "grand Monster Tennessean." When exhibited in Nashville in December 1845, the mastodon remains were mounted upright beside an articulated human skeleton for scale. After James X. Corgan and Emmanuel Breitburg, *Tennessee's Prehistoric Vertebrates*, Tennessee Division of Geology Bulletin 84 (Nashville: State of Tennessee Department of Environment and Conservation, 1996), fig. 1.

the skeleton was billed not as an ancient elephant, but rather as the remains of an Antediluvian giant human (Figure 1.1).⁴ The "grand Monster Tennessean" was first displayed at the old courthouse in Franklin, where the price of admission was set at twenty-five cents. The skeleton then moved north to Nashville in December of 1845, where it was installed alongside an average-size human skeleton. Due to popular demand, the price of admission increased to thirty cents, though with a 50 percent discount for servants and children. From Nashville, the exhibit embarked on a tour to New Orleans, where the fraud was quickly recognized by a medical professor. The skeleton disappeared from public view, although not before convincing thousands of visitors that the Nashville area was once home to an ancient race of giant humans.

It is not unusual for those digging holes in Middle Tennessee to uncover pieces of the deep past. Historical documents from the nineteenth and early twentieth centuries record what seems to be a near-continuous stream of encounters with ancient remains. Those range from accidental fossil discoveries such as the Shumate Mastodon to deliberate excavations of ancient Native American sites by antiquarian scholars from the likes of Harvard's Peabody Museum. In the middle of that spectrum fell the interested public of Nashville and Middle Tennessee, some of whom spent their leisure time collecting fossils or digging up Native American sites in search of artifacts and curiosities. This trend continues today, as Nashville's growing population and associated development expand throughout Middle Tennessee and spur both formal archaeological studies and accidental encounters with the past.

During the first decades of the twenty-first century there have been occasional, brief peaks of public interest in our city's deep past. These are typically in response to ancient Native American sites being threatened or impacted by development efforts, such as the large May Town Center project proposed for Bells Bend in 2008, or construction of the new Nashville Sounds stadium in 2014. For the most part, however, the city's ancient past has remained a mere footnote to its antebellum and more recent history.

Aside from the good work of the Tennessee State Museum and occasional roadside historical markers, the popular interpretation and treatment of ancient Nashville has been driven mainly by curiosity and imagination rather than modern science. Without the benefit of responsible, accessible sources, explanations of Nashville's deep past have over the years included tales about lost races of giants and pygmies, various ancient Old World cultures, and "the Moundbuilders," an outdated nineteenth-century term for the Native Americans who created North America's first monumental architecture. On the other hand, sources written for schoolchildren, and those for a more general public audience, might lead us to believe that the first Europeans arrived on the banks of the Cumberland River in the late seventeenth century to find a pristine landscape, inhabited only by herds of bison and boundless nature, entirely untouched by human hands.

Just three short centuries before Illinois lieutenant-governor-turned-fur-trader Timothy Demonbreun set foot at Sulphur Dell, Native American communities belonging to what archaeologists identify as the Middle Cumberland Mississippian culture lived throughout the Cumberland River watershed in Middle Tennessee. The French Lick area, today home to Bicentennial Mall State Park and the Nashville Sounds baseball stadium, was the site of a densely populated town. Homes, private and public spaces, cemeteries, and salt processing areas filled the valley of Lick Branch, while an earthen mound built near the river would later serve as the foundation for the French fort and fur trading post.[5] On the opposite bank of the Cumberland, in the area where Top Golf now stands, a series of earthen mounds held ritual structures and the homes and graves of high-status individuals. The large village that surrounded those mounds extended north toward Cleveland Park and east along the river toward Shelby Bottoms. These sites were not isolated, but were part of a tapestry of towns, villages, and farms that stretched for miles across the Nashville landscape and into neighboring Williamson, Sumner, and Cheatham Counties.

Just as they predate the French arrival in Nashville, Mississippian period sites do not represent the first human presence in Middle Tennessee. Rather, the archaeological roots of Music City include the entire scope of human activity in the region, extending at least 13,000 years back to the last ice age. The paleontological record of Nashville extends even further, reaching millions of years back into geologic time. It is this cumulative layer-cake of history, the stories told by fossils and artifacts, by sabertooth cats and Native American communities, on which modern Nashville is built.

The First Nashvillians

The first people to set foot in Middle Tennessee arrived in the Cumberland River Valley approximately 13,000 years ago. Over ensuing millennia those ancient Native Americans and their descendants left behind a record that archaeologists divide into four broad cultural periods: the Paleoindian, Archaic, Woodland, and Mississippian. No system of writing or record keeping has survived from this archaeological past. We do not know how these communities identified themselves, what language(s) they spoke, or what names they gave to their towns and settlements. Instead, the four archaeological periods are separated from one another based on gradual culture changes including shifting artifact technologies, diets, settlement types, and social organization.

The Paleoindian period begins with the arrival of the first people in North America, during the end of the Pleistocene geologic epoch. These settlers are known to archaeologists as the First Americans, and as their descendants arrived along the Cumberland, gradual climate shifts accompanying the end of the last ice age had begun to accelerate. The resulting environmental changes impacted both plant and animal communities and contributed to the eventual extinction of large, cold-adapted animals known as megafauna. Nevertheless, the first Tennesseans shared the late ice age landscape with, and sometimes hunted (or not, as we'll see in Chapter 3), now-extinct creatures such as the mastodon.

Following the retreat of Pleistocene glacial ice, Earth transitioned to the Holocene, our contemporary geologic epoch. From about 8000 through 1000 BC, numerous Archaic period groups inhabited the greater Nashville landscape. The area's population increased dramatically during this time, as bands composed of multiple extended families hunted and foraged along the rivers of Middle Tennessee. Native Americans also began to experiment with food production over the long span of the Archaic period. They domesticated plants including squash, sunflower, and goosefoot, and as described in Chapter 4, perhaps managed freshwater shellfish beds in the Cumberland and its tributaries. These groups also took part in long-distance trade networks and began to acquire objects from outside of Middle Tennessee, such as artifacts made from large whelk shells originating along the Gulf of Mexico.

The Woodland period follows the Archaic, as between about 1000 BC and AD 1000 Native American communities gradually settled into long-term villages and began to practice household gardening and intensive horticulture. During the Woodland period the construction of earthen mounds, use of ceramic vessels, and bow and arrow technology, all of which developed elsewhere in North America thousands of years earlier, gradually became widespread throughout Tennessee. It was also during this period that Native American groups began to organize into socially stratified societies, connected through both trade and ideology to Woodland period communities in other regions, including the Hopewell and Adena cultures of the Ohio Valley.

For reasons that remain unclear, Nashville-area populations seem to have dispersed during the Woodland period. People continued to live along the Cumberland River and its tributaries, but with just a few exceptions, major occupations in Middle Tennessee shifted south to the Duck River watershed. The principal exception to this trend was the Glass Mounds site, located in Williamson County west of Franklin. That site along the West Harpeth River once included multiple earthen mounds, and based on artifacts recovered during the late nineteenth century appears to have had direct connections to, or major influence from, the Hopewell culture of the Ohio Valley.[6] The Glass Mounds site was almost entirely destroyed by phosphate mining during the mid-twentieth century, and Woodland period Nashville remains poorly understood.

By the eleventh century AD, Native American societies in the Nashville area and throughout the Eastern Woodlands transitioned into highly ranked communities of the Mississippian period. In Chapter 5, we describe the Mississippian settlements that flourished along the rivers of Middle Tennessee between around AD 1000 and 1475. The Mississippian period is perhaps best known today for its large towns, in which homes and cemeteries were organized around groups of earthen mounds that, depending on their design, served both living and deceased members of the upper class.

Skilled Mississippian artisans produced beautiful and enduring objects in ceramic, stone, and shell, for both everyday and ritual use. Trade networks, along with political and religious influences, connected the Middle Cumberland Mississippian culture to Native American societies throughout eastern North America. Mississippian period people continued to fish, hunt, and gather wild resources, but primarily made their living by intensive farming of maize, beans, and other crops. Mississippian culture ended in Middle Tennessee during the mid-fifteenth century following decades of droughts and political upheaval. Although a number of Native American tribes continued to periodically enter the region after that time, archaeological evidence for permeant human occupation in greater Nashville is virtually absent between about AD 1475 and the late seventeenth century.

In accordance with federal and state laws, the Tennessee Division of Archaeology maintains a database of known archaeological and paleontological sites within the borders of the state. As of spring 2021, there are nearly 700 site locations officially recorded in Davidson

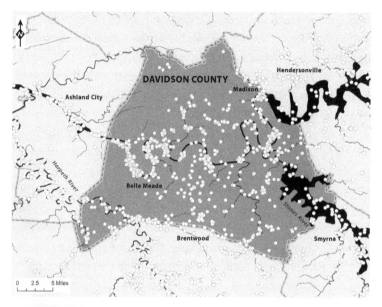

FIGURE I.2. Map of archaeological and paleontological sites in and surrounding Davidson County.

County (Figure 1.2). More than 480 of these include artifacts or fossils originating before AD 1500 and are considered *prehistoric*. This term is not a value judgement as to the complexity of ancient Tennesseans, but instead means simply that these sites predate the arrival of written texts in the American Southeast.

Beyond Davidson County, the overall number of prehistoric sites in the greater Nashville area includes more than 330 in Williamson County, over 200 each in Rutherford and Sumner Counties, and around 180 in Cheatham County. These numbers do not reflect the sum total of prehistoric sites in Middle Tennessee, but rather those which have been officially recorded with the Division of Archaeology. "New" sites are constantly encountered as suburban growth expands into previously rural lands throughout the Nashville area. In Davidson County alone, more than thirty sites were recorded between 2015 and 2020.

How Archaeologists Learn about the Past

The archaeological record of Nashville includes all of the evidence of at least 13,000 years of human culture, beginning at the level of the individual artifact. Public interest in ancient Native American artifacts typically focuses on those objects that are collectible, or displayed in museums: whole stone tools, ceramic pots, statues, and artwork. For archaeologists, however, artifacts include every single object modified or used by humans, from the most intricately carved shell pendant to the smallest microscopic plant remains. Beyond these materials the archaeological record also includes features, which mark past human activities and are sometimes defined as "non-portable arti-facts." At the functional level, features include things like hearths or ovens, graves, and the remains of structures. Artifacts and features combine to create archaeological sites, which in turn combine to form human-made landscapes such as the Middle Cumberland Mississippian occupations of Middle Tennessee.

Artifacts and fossils are not the same thing. While artifacts are the result of human activity, fossils are the petrified remains of once-living creatures. Throughout human history, people have encountered and collected fossils, sometimes altering or adapting them for use or display. As a result, those fossils also become artifacts. As with the First American Cave site described in Chapter 2, fossils and artifacts are sometimes found at the same locations, and their stories become intertwined. Ultimately though, they are different things, represent different parts of the past, and are studied by different scientists. Archaeologists don't dig dinosaurs, although we sometimes get to excavate a sabertooth cat or ice age elephant.

Nashville's deep past is constantly under threat of destruction by both natural and human forces. Floods, erosion, farming, develop-ment, artifact collecting, and even archaeological excavation all destroy sites. Every hole dug and every artifact or fossil taken away from its original setting without a record of its provenience—the exact location where it was recovered relative to the overall site—is like removing random puzzle pieces from a box, individually framing them, and hanging them on the wall for display. Without the entire box, those pieces of the puzzle are reduced to mere objects. Individual artifacts, like those few framed puzzle pieces, show us colorful bits of a much larger picture. They may be aesthetically pleasing but cannot tell us much about people's lives in the past.

To fully appreciate the interlocking mosaic of the puzzle as a whole, we must work deliberately with time-tested methods and techniques. There is a method to putting together a puzzle: start with the edges. So it is with archaeology. Professional archaeologists use methods and techniques developed and refined over generations, honed under the watchful eye of professional mentors, so they can methodically collect not just aesthetically pleasing artifacts, but also the data necessary to reconstruct past environments and lifeways. Modern research-driven archaeology includes complete collection and detailed analysis of even the smallest artifact remains, as well as exhaustive site documentation. Even those aspects of a site that do not immediately appear to be significant must be documented in minute detail to allow for future interpretation and analysis. It is only through this approach that we can offset the loss to our shared history that comes with excavation. Far from being a rollicking adventure in the search of ancient mysteries and museum-quality specimens, modern archaeology is painfully detail oriented. None of our colleagues wear fedoras or carry bullwhips, and only a few can boast of having French nemeses or punching Nazis.

To get a better idea of how the different types of archaeological data combine to tell us about the past, consider the first project we worked on together. We began collaborating on archaeological research in 2007, soon after being introduced at the Current Research in Tennessee Archaeology meeting. That annual event is organized by the Tennessee Division of Archaeology and the Middle Tennessee State University (MTSU) Department of Sociology and Anthropology, and includes a day of free presentations by professional archaeologists and students describing their recent research on Tennessee's archaeological past. We had both recently started new jobs, Aaron at the Division of Archaeology, and Tanya at MTSU, and were both interested in opportunities to engage undergraduates in archaeological research. That year we, along with our colleague Shannon Hodge, a bioarchaeologist and professor at Middle Tennessee State University, undertook a collaborative effort to examine a large collection of unanalyzed artifacts and data previously recovered from a site along the South Harpeth River in Williamson County.

The Fernvale archaeological site was excavated by the Division of Archaeology in the 1980s ahead of a road and bridge construction project, but neither the artifact analysis nor the project report were ever completed.[7] With the aid of the site archive, including feature excavation logs, daily excavator journals, photographs, written communications, and even budget records, we were able to reconstruct the project trajectory and better understand the site as a whole. Over nearly seven years we worked together with Hodge and a series of MTSU anthropology undergraduates to examine, classify, and catalog every artifact from the site, ultimately compiling all of our data into a technical report. That document included detailed information on the site setting, history of excavations, and discussions of all the artifacts as well as information on their original locations relative to the overall site plan. Technical reports are not particularly interesting to read for the layperson, but they provide information critical to understanding the site and to future research.

Radiocarbon dates and diagnostic artifacts, those items that can be confidently assigned a particular age range based on their physical characteristics, showed the Fernvale site was periodically home to Native Americans for a period of over 9,000 years. The earliest portion of that time span was represented by just a few stone spear points, left behind by one or a few hunter-gatherer-foragers who lived in the area around 8000 BC. The most recent portion of the site consisted of a Mississippian period farmstead, including the footprint of a single-family home and several outbuildings dated to around AD 1130.

The most intensive occupation at the Fernvale site took place during the Late Archaic period, between about 4000 and 1000 BC. During that time the site was not permanently settled, but instead was used as a regular, seasonal campsite. Beneath the uppermost levels of disturbed soils, known to archaeologists as the plowzone, excavators uncovered dark, circular stains marking the footprints of nearly two hundred pit features. These were the result of holes being dug into the earth, which were used for a variety of daily needs such as to discard trash, store items, cook, or in some cases, bury the dead. Ultimately excavations within the road and bridge footprint uncovered more than 101,000 individual artifacts, including stone, animal bone, freshwater shell, seed and nut fragments, wood charcoal, and the graves of thirty-two individuals.

The number of artifacts excavated at the Fernvale site seems impressive on its face, but more than 80 percent of the collection consisted simply of debitage: flint flakes mostly smaller than a half inch across, left over from making or sharpening stone tools. Only around six hundred of the total artifacts from the site were finished stone or bone tools, and fewer than one hundred of those were unbroken. This was not a "museum quality" site. Nevertheless, by carefully examining the entirety of the collected archaeological data, we were able to learn a great deal about the people who lived along the South Harpeth River during the Late Archaic period.

Burned remains of plant seeds and nuts collected from within features demonstrate that Native Americans camped at this location mainly in the late summer through early winter. During those times they collected wild plant foods including walnuts, hazelnuts, acorns, honey locust seed pods, grapes, and goosefoot. Careful analysis of animal bones from the site reveal that they hunted local animals including white-tailed deer, turkey and other birds, various small mammals, reptiles, and amphibians.

The families who lived at the site did so alongside their domesticated dogs, and the burials of several of those animals show us something of the human-canine relationship. In one case, a mature dog was placed in the grave of an older woman. The dog lay curled behind the woman's back, with its head resting on her shoulder and right forepaw tucked under her arm. While this clearly shows that dogs were important as companions, we also know they were working animals who accompanied hunting groups and assisted with other daily tasks. Deformed vertebrae along the spinal column of one dog buried at the site show that while alive that animal regularly carried loads on its back, probably as a pack or while pulling a sled-like travois.[8]

There was little evidence that the occupants of the Fernvale site engaged in trade beyond the South Harpeth watershed. Nearly all of the animal remains and the stones used to make their tools came from the local environment, with one significant exception. One shallow pit feature at the site was virtually empty of artifacts except for a four-inch wide circular shell gorget. That neck ornament was carved from the outer whorl of a marine lightning whelk and was undecorated other than a hole drilled in the center (Figure 1.3). The gorget was placed in the feature atop a stack of fifty-one shell beads, also made from marine whelk and mostly measuring smaller than ¼-inch. The shells from which these artifacts were made probably originated along the Florida Gulf Coast, and radiocarbon dating determined the gorget to be nearly 2,000 years older than the associated beads.[9] There are other, earlier Archaic period sites in both Middle

FIGURE 1.3. Archaic period marine shell gorget and beads from the Fernvale site. These were found stacked together in a small pit feature that contained virtually no other artifacts. They were strung together on cotton twine in the 1980s by the original excavators. Photograph courtesy of the Tennessee Division of Archaeology.

Tennessee and central Kentucky with evidence of marine shells, and it is possible the Fernvale gorget was an heirloom curated and passed on for many generations.

Analysis of the human skeletal remains from the Fernvale site showed a 27 percent mortality rate for children and infants.[10] That seems staggering by modern standards but is not an unusual statistic for historical populations prior to the twentieth century.[11] Most of the adults buried at the site died between thirty and fifty years of age, with only two individuals possibly reaching age sixty. There were several examples of healed broken ribs and an ankle, but no evidence of violent death or healed traumatic injuries resulting from interpersonal violence. That said, two burials at the site exhibited trauma consistent with dismemberment. The evidence points to these individuals having had both arms, and possibly their heads, deliberately removed with stone tools at or around the time of death. The partial dismemberments may be related to what archaeologists call "trophy taking," a practice that has been documented at other sites in the greater American Southeast.[12] These "trophies" may in fact be relics, which are important in many ancient religions around the world. As such, they relate to the veneration of revered ancestors or some other poorly understood religious or ritual activity.

The information that can be gleaned from archaeological collections is not limited to a single analysis effort. Instead, new technologies and methods are constantly evolving which allow us to reevaluate and better understand both sites and artifacts. Nearly a decade after beginning work on the Fernvale collection, we used high-tech analysis of artifacts from the site to identify a previously unknown aspect of Archaic period Native American culture: tattooing.

The original excavations at the Fernvale site recovered two sharpened turkey bone awls alongside a group of other stone, bone, and shell artifacts dated to between about 1600 and 3500 BC. We were curious to learn if the turkey bone tools were used to pierce leather, or perhaps for some other purpose, and so used high-powered digital microscopes to examine the wear patterns on their tips. When a tool is used, whether today or in the past, that action creates microscopic wear patterns on its surfaces. Those patterns build up and become more distinctive over time and can be "read" to learn specific information about how and against what material the tool was wielded. For example, a stone tool used to carve wood will show different microwear patterns than an identically shaped tool used to cut wood or plant fibers, or to slice meat.

We determined that the wear patterns on the tips of the two turkey bone awls matched those documented during experimental studies using bone tools to tattoo.[13] We also identified microscopic traces of black and red pigments on the tips of the awls, and through elemental analysis determined that iron oxide was the main component of the red pigments. Until this discovery, there was no definitive evidence of Native American tattooing in eastern North America prior to the sixteenth century AD. Unfortunately, no artistic depictions of marked human bodies survive from the Late Archaic, and therefore we do not know what the tattoos themselves looked like. In addition to illuminating a previously unknown Archaic period practice in Tennessee, the artifacts from Fernvale are also significant in that they are, to our knowledge, the world's oldest proven tattoo tools.

A Brief History of Early Nashville Archaeology

As you see, we can learn some tremendous details about the past by studying the complete archaeological record of a site. Unfortunately, it was not until the latter half of the twentieth century that investigations of Nashville's deep past were conducted in a scientific, responsible manner. Some of the earliest and largest excavations of Native American archaeological sites in Middle Tennessee were undertaken during the nineteenth century by antiquarian scholars. These learned individuals were interested in the historical record, but most were not trained as archaeologists and all were subject to the biases and attitudes of the time in which they lived. Several of them may have worn fedoras.

In Middle Tennessee, the antiquarian community included notable figures such as Judge Haywood; Tennessee's first state geologist, Gerard Troost; Nashville health officer Joseph Jones; Ralph E. W. Earl, the founder of Tennessee's first museum; and Union general Gates P. Thruston. The earthen mounds and Mississippian period cemeteries of Middle Tennessee also attracted outside attention, including from representatives of the Smithsonian Institution and the Peabody Museum at Harvard University, who were dispatched to Nashville in pursuit of artifacts to add to their institutions' fledgling collections.

These wealthy men and their contemporaries hired local laborers to dig up dozens of Mississippian mound and cemetery sites throughout the Nashville area in search of burial items and exhibition-quality objects. Unfortunately, they had little interest in incomplete or less aesthetically pleasing artifacts, which they typically discarded, and kept few records as to where within a site any specific artifact was found. Jones and several others did in some cases conduct research-driven studies of Mississippian period skeletal remains, particularly as related to claims that there had once existed a society of ancient Tennessee "pygmies."[14] However, in keeping with the attitudes of the day, little interest was devoted to the daily lifeways and experiences of the people who lived at the sites, and no consideration at all was paid to the majority of the population, who did not live atop mounds or bury their dead with fancy objects. In this regard, the early archaeology of Nashville was fundamentally not much different than contemporaneous antiquarian work taking place in Egypt or Mesopotamia.

Perhaps the earliest scientific archaeology in Middle Tennessee was done by Vanderbilt University graduate and self-trained archaeologist William Edward Myer. Beginning in the late 1800s, Myer investigated numerous archaeological sites throughout the Nashville area, including the Mississippian mound sites of Castalian Springs in Sumner County, the Mound Bottom and Pack sites in Cheatham County, and Fewkes Mounds in Brentwood.[15] In 1917-1918 he attempted the first statewide archaeological survey, and from 1919 until his death in 1923 he served as Tennessee's unofficial state archaeologist while also working with the Smithsonian Institution's Bureau of American

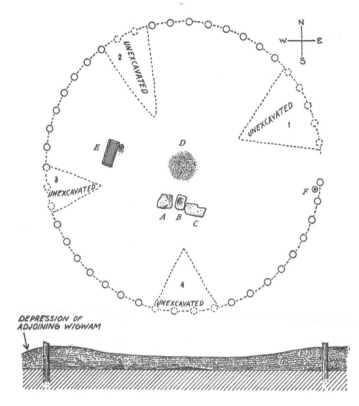

FIGURE 1.4. William Edward Myer's sketch of a Mississippian period house excavated at the Gordontown village site in Brentwood: (A–C) groundstone mortars found in place on the house floor, (D) the central hearth, (E) stone box grave of a child located beneath the house floor, (F) ceramic vessel resting on the house floor. Circles around the exterior show the locations of postmold features forming the outer wall of the house. After William E. Myer, "Two Prehistoric Villages in Middle Tennessee," in *Forty-first Annual Report of the American Bureau of Ethnology to the Secretary of the Smithsonian Institution, 1919–1924*, ed. J. Walter Fewkes (Washington, DC: US Government Printing Office, 1928), Fig. 150.

Ethnology.[16] Some of the objects Myer excavated in Middle Tennessee ultimately ended up in the collections of the National Museum of American History and the National Museum of the American Indian.

Myer's work stands out from earlier antiquarian scholars in that, rather than focusing on the recovery of burial objects, he was interested in documenting and understanding the details of earthen mounds, structures, and village middens (Figure 1.4). This led him to carefully document overall site plans and soil profiles within his excavations. Myer was thereby able to identify construction sequences within mounds and demonstrate that earthworks and structures were often rebuilt or added to over time. He also collected a wide variety of artifact types during his excavations. Myer's work includes some of the earliest efforts to identify archaeological animal bones according to species, and to try and interpret what those remains revealed about diets in the past.

The year following Myer's death, Governor Austin Peay appointed Parmenio E. Cox as the first official state archaeologist. Cox would go on to create the first Tennessee Archaeological Society, but he was more dedicated to the promotion of archaeology than to responsible excavation practices. Cox kept few records of his work and curated only artifacts in which he was personally interested. Many of those objects, along with others donated to Cox during his tenure as state archaeologist, ended up in the collection of the Tennessee Historical Society and ultimately the Tennessee State Museum.

Most archaeological work in Nashville during the mid-twentieth century was done by a strong community of avocational archaeologists. These individuals came from various walks of life, and while most did not have anthropology degrees or formal archaeological training, all were interested in the documentation and preservation of ancient Nashville. In 1963, Nashville's avocational community worked together to charter the Southeastern Indian Antiquities Survey (SIAS), one of the first organizations to promote active preservation of Nashville's deep past.[17] This was done through a combination of public programming, partnerships with Vanderbilt University and several Native American tribes, and publication of journals including the *Choctaw Times*.

SIAS members including Buddy Brehm, John Dowd, and Bob Ferguson (who we will meet again in Chapter 2) recorded the first, and in many cases only, information on numerous archaeological sites in Middle Tennessee. Vanderbilt University's Department of Anthropology provided meeting space for the SIAS, and during the 1960s and 1970s Vanderbilt professor Ronald Spores and some of his students participated in various SIAS field projects. This partnership was brief, however, and with the exception of doctoral research by Kevin Smith, now a professor of anthropology at MTSU, Vanderbilt's archaeology program has focused more on Central and South America than on local Native American archaeology and culture.

The Recent Past

For nearly four decades following the death of P. E. Cox there was no official state archaeologist in Tennessee, and no state organization tasked with overseeing Tennessee's archaeological heritage. Thanks in part to lobbying efforts of the SIAS, this changed in 1970 with the passage of the Tennessee Antiquities Act, under which the Tennessee Division of Archaeology was officially established as part of the Department of Conservation.[18] In 1971, Governor Winfield Dunn appointed Mack Prichard, a biologist by training, to the position of Tennessee's first modern state archaeologist. Prichard oversaw the formation of the Division of Archaeology, before moving on to become Tennessee's first state naturalist. Throughout the 1970s and 1980s, Division of Archaeology staff conducted research and excavations on state-owned sites such as the Mound Bottom and Sellars Farm State Archaeological Areas, as well as excavation projects at sites like Fernvale on behalf of the Tennessee Department of Transportation.

During the late twentieth century, archaeology in Middle Tennessee underwent a major shift with the passage of federal preservation laws. Today most archaeological work in the United States is completed according to the requirements of the National Historic

Preservation Act of 1966. Essentially, any undertaking that uses federal monies or requires permitting by a federal agency must conduct archaeological studies to identify and evaluate any archaeological resources situated within a planned project area. Under this process, significant sites must be either avoided or mitigated, which typically means being carefully excavated by professional archaeologists employed by private cultural resource management firms. However, while the National Historic Preservation Act laid the groundwork for these studies, archaeology was not a main focus for implementation of the law until the mid-1970s.

One of the first archaeological efforts undertaken in Nashville under the National Historic Preservation Act was at the Averbuch site, a Mississippian period village located in the Bordeaux neighborhood. In 1975, earthmoving for a new residential subdivision unexpectedly disturbed several ancient Native American graves within planned residential lots. The Division of Archaeology conducted preliminary investigations at the site with the assistance of local volunteers, and identified the remains of several Mississippian homes and a cemetery containing nearly fifty graves.

The development project was financed under loan guarantees from the Federal Housing Administration, thereby triggering archaeological study under the National Historic Preservation Act. From 1977 to 1978, the Department of the Interior provided funds to hire archaeologists from the University of Tennessee to recover endangered archaeological data at the Averbuch site. That work ultimately investigated only a small fraction of the seven-acre village, which was surrounded by a defensive palisade wall and included dozens of houses, as well as three cemeteries containing a total of more than one thousand burials.[19] Approximately a third of the site had been entirely destroyed by construction activity prior to any archaeological investigation.

In 1976, Nick Fielder joined the Tennessee Historical Commission in Nashville as their federal programs reviewer. Fielder grew up in Oak Ridge, Tennessee, and until the late 1960s worked as an engineer for Boeing and NASA. He returned to Tennessee in 1969 as a photographer on the Tellico Archaeological Project, investigating dozens of sites in the Little Tennessee River Valley before going on to earn degrees in anthropology from the University of Tennessee, Knoxville and the University of Idaho.

In 1980, Fielder was appointed as the Tennessee State Archaeologist in the then-Department of Conservation, a role in which he would serve until 2007. During his tenure the population of greater Nashville grew by nearly 80 percent,[20] and widespread urban and commercial expansion began to impact the archaeological record of Middle Tennessee at an unprecedented level. Archaeological sites and artifacts located on private property in Tennessee receive no special protections under state or federal law except where federal permitting is involved, and a tremendous amount of archaeological data was lost or destroyed during the initial boom of twentieth-century development.

Today human burials in Tennessee are protected by state cemetery laws that shield all human graves, burial monuments, and associated artifacts from deliberate disturbance.[21] However, these protections were not extended to Native American burials until the mid-1980s. Prior to that time there was no formal, legal precedent preventing excavation of, or vandalism to, Native American graves. As a result, hundreds of ancient Native American cemeteries were disturbed or destroyed during Nashville's twentieth-century suburban growth.

The state burial statutes were updated in 1990 to include additional protections for Native American burials, including prohibitions against the exhibition of Native American skeletal remains, and the requirement that the public inform the coroner, medical examiner, and local law enforcement in the event that human remains are accidentally encountered. Under Tennessee's cemetery laws developers or landowners may, with an order from the Chancery Court, hire a mortician or private archaeological company to identify and remove abandoned or neglected cemeteries on their property. Those burials are typically reinterred elsewhere, according to the terms of the court order. Unfortunately, neither landowners nor their representatives are legally obligated to avoid or document any archaeological features that do not contain graves, and there is no required oversight for burial removal projects, except according to the good will of the developer. Thankfully under Fielder's leadership, the Division of Archaeology was able to negotiate permission to document and conduct salvage excavations at several major Mississippian sites in and around Nashville during court-ordered burial removal projects.

Such was the case with the Brentwood Library site, which was unexpectedly rediscovered in 1997. Following the accidental unearthing of numerous Mississippian period graves, the city of Brentwood was granted a court order and hired a private consultant to identify and remove all burials from within the planned library footprint. While that work was taking place, the Division of Archaeology was granted permission, with assistance of volunteers from MTSU and local avocational societies, to document thousands of non-burial features including house footprints, cooking hearths, storage and trash pits, and part of a defensive palisade wall.[22] That effort salvaged a tremendous amount of archaeological data that would otherwise have been lost, and as described in Chapter 5, helped launch research that would reshape our understanding of Mississippian societies in the Nashville area.

Today there are dozens of archaeologists living and working in the Nashville area, including those with the Division of Archaeology, Tennessee Department of Transportation, US Army Corps of Engineers, Middle Tennessee State University, Vanderbilt University, and several for-profit cultural resource management firms. Many of these individuals are part of the Tennessee Council for Professional Archaeology, which was founded in 1992 as Tennessee's only statewide

The Tennessee State Artifact is part of the collection of the McClung Museum of Natural History and Culture at the University of Tennessee-Knoxville, where he is displayed in the permanent exhibition "Archaeology and the Native Peoples of Tennessee."

Tennessee Council for Professional Archaeology and Tennessee Historical Commission

FIGURE 1.5. The postcard version of the 2015 Tennessee Archaeology Awareness Month poster, featuring Tennessee's state artifact: a Mississippian period statue from Sellars Farm State Archaeological Area. Photograph by David H. Dye; poster design by Noël Lorson.

archaeological interest organization. From 2014 to 2016, under Tanya's leadership as president, the organization successfully lobbied for legislation naming September as Tennessee Archaeology Awareness Month, and also designating Tennessee's official state artifact: an eighteen-inch tall Mississippian period stone statue that today resides in Knoxville's McClung Museum of Natural History and Culture (Figure 1.5). That statue was discovered in 1939 by a tenant farmer working land that is now part of Sellars Farm State Archaeological Area in Wilson County, and is one of four stone statues from the site. Archaeologists believe these artifacts, which seem to have been made as male-female pairs, represent ancestral figures, and perhaps the founders of hereditary lineages that controlled power in Mississippian towns.[23]

Anniversaries are a good time to pause and reflect on the years and events that led us to the milestone we wish to mark. As we race, or in some cases stumble, toward modern Nashville's 250th anniversary, we should take the time to consider the deep history of this place we love and that so many people, past and present, have called home. The stories in this book cover thousands of years, from before humans camped along the banks of the Cumberland to the relatively recent construction of earthen mounds that dot the Middle Tennessee landscape. Our goal is to give you, the reader, a better understanding of Nashville's deep past, including the scope of ancient Native American history in Nashville, the role of archaeologists and the public in documenting and preserving the record of the past, and some of the more enigmatic local discoveries, people, sites, and traditions that are not well known outside of professional circles. There are too many stories, too many characters, and too many unanticipated discoveries in unearthing and understanding Nashville's deep past. We couldn't possibly do justice to all of these in a single book of this size, so instead we offer up four of the more iconic stories on our list that give you a small taste of the Nashville that came before.

CHAPTER 2

The Nashville Cat

"Hockey is for everyone!" booms Paul Weber's voice from the Bridgestone Arena sound system, just minutes before the puck drops at the Nashville Predators' latest home match. "Even for prehistoric *Smilodons!*" On cue the Predator's mascot, Gnash, a blue and white sabertooth cat outfitted in a hockey jersey, launches himself from the tunnel and slides across the rink, waving his arms and bringing the crowd to their feet. The sabertooth tiger has become a Nashville icon, thanks to our hometown National Hockey League franchise. For seven months out of the year, longer if the team plays well, the head of a snarling ice age cat, in profile, is seen throughout the city on banners and billboards and proudly worn on jerseys, hats, and scarves wound around the necks of locals and tourists alike. The Predators and their logo have become an essential part of Nashville's identity, to the point that—at least for eighty-two nights a year—it could be argued we are less Music City than Smashville.

The Predators logo, the official team history, and Gnash's origin story all reference the 1971 discovery of a sabertooth cat skeleton in a cave located beneath downtown Nashville. Today some of those bones are even on display in the Bridgestone Arena for fans to see first-hand. Nevertheless, despite the popularity of the Predators and their mascot, the full story of Nashville's sabertooth cat discovery remains mostly unknown.

Nashville's fortunes and population were on the rise as the city entered the second half of the twentieth century. New homes, roads, and businesses created to accommodate a rapidly growing population pushed into areas that had, until just years before, retained a rural character. At the same time, city-sponsored initiatives were busy with urban redevelopment and the demolition of older buildings and neighborhoods in the downtown core, all to pave the way for the "New Nashville."[1]

There was no meaningful legal protection or oversight for Davidson County's archaeological and paleontological sites during this period of urban growth. As we described in Chapter 1, the Tennessee Division of Archaeology was not officially established until 1970 following passage of the Tennessee Antiquities Act, and state cemetery laws did not yet apply to Native American graves. Instead, preservation and documentation of Nashville's archaeological record was left in the hands of a group of talented avocational archaeologists, including RCA Records producer Bob Ferguson.

Ferguson was a man of many talents. During the 1960s as a senior producer with RCA Victor, Ferguson worked on records by country music luminaries including Dolly Parton, Chet Atkins, and Porter Wagoner.[2] He was also a songwriter, penning hits including "Carroll County Accident," which was awarded the Country Music Association Song of the Year for 1969. Beyond his prodigious musical talent, Ferguson had a strong interest in Native American history inspired both by his wife Martha's Choctaw heritage and Tennessee's ancient Native American sites. It was this interest that led Ferguson to earn his master's degree in anthropology from Vanderbilt University while working for RCA. He went on to volunteer his time alongside a community of avocational archaeologists who worked to identify and record ancient Native American sites throughout Middle Tennessee and salvage archaeological data from sites threatened by new development. Those efforts led to the formation of the Southeastern

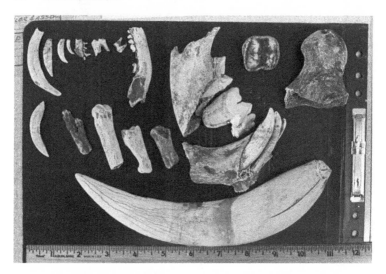

FIGURE 2.1. Animal bones recovered from the First American Bank site on August 12, 1971. Parts of the sabertooth jaw are in the middle of the frame, above the iconic fang. Original photograph by Les Leverett.

Indian Antiquities Survey (SIAS), of which Ferguson was a founding member and the first President.[3]

August 12, 1971, found Ferguson in Hendersonville at the House of Cash, where he was to collect a $10,000 donation from the Man in Black to help underwrite the SIAS. "As Johnny signed the check for presentation," Ferguson later recalled, "the telephone rang."[4] The call was for Ferguson, and on the other end of the line was the public relations manager for First American National Bank. The bank had recently begun construction on new headquarters at the corner of Third Avenue and Deaderick Street, overlooking Public Square in downtown Nashville. Earlier that day workers clearing blasted limestone bedrock for the building foundations had made a surprising discovery: bones in the bucket of a power shovel. They believed the find might have archaeological importance, and so had contacted Vanderbilt's Department of Anthropology, who referred them to Ferguson.[5] On reaching the downtown construction office Ferguson was presented with a collection of skeletal material, among which he immediately recognized both human and animal remains, including a nine-inch-long fang from a sabertooth cat (Figure 2.1).

Excavating the First American Cave

After viewing the bones, Ferguson, other members of the SIAS, and representatives from the First American Bank inspected the construction site. About twenty to thirty feet below the modern ground surface they identified the source of the remains: a mud- and clay-filled cavity that had been exposed by blasting and mechanical excavation. This was, Ferguson realized, the remnants of a cave that had been mostly destroyed during removal of the limestone bedrock.

A portion of the cavity appeared to still be intact, and the bank agreed to let the SIAS investigate the site further. The archaeological team worked around the construction schedule each afternoon and on weekends to sort through what SIAS member John Dowd would later remember as a "churned up mess."[6] In addition to carefully excavating and sifting soil from the cave remnants, the crew combed through spoil piles where construction debris had been dumped.

The excavations ultimately recovered several hundred bones, including both human and animal remains. The human bones were from several ancient Native American graves, remnants of which were still situated near the top of the cave, approximately sixteen feet above the sabertooth cat. Based on their arrangement, bundled and placed alongside one another in a parallel fashion, excavators suggested that the burials were from the Woodland period (ca. 1000 BC–AD 1000). This conclusion was borne out when subsequent radiocarbon dating of two human tibias—a destructive process which would not even be considered today—returned an age range of between approximately 510 BC and AD 345.[7]

After eight or nine weeks, bank construction could no longer avoid the cave area, and excavations were halted. The SIAS study had determined that approximately seven feet of undisturbed deposits likely

remained intact below the level of the excavation, and the bank ultimately agreed to avoid and preserve the remaining area by constructing the building foundations around it.[8] That work was completed by
the summer of 1972, and a metal ladder and hatch were installed to
access the space from the bank's parking garage. At the time it was
reported that excavations would soon recommence within the cave.[9]
For unknown reasons that work never took place, and no archaeologist would again visit the cave site until 2008.

Because only a small portion of the cave remained following
discovery of the bones, the original size and extent of the cavern
were not clear. At the time no cave mouth or opening was known to
exist in the area, and investigators suggested that the chamber had
once connected to the surface via a sinkhole or crevasse. Perhaps the
sabertooth and other animals had fallen into a near-vertical fissure
and been unable to escape, although the deliberately placed Native
American graves suggested the chamber was, at least later in its history, connected to a passable entrance.

Downtown Caves and Crevasses in Nashville History

The discovery of the cave beneath the First American Bank was
wholly unanticipated in 1971. However, just a century earlier subterranean crevasses were known to honeycomb the bedrock of downtown Nashville (Figure 2.2). Local newspaper stories from the late
nineteenth and early twentieth centuries describe encounters with
underground caverns during construction throughout the downtown
core, including at the original City Hall, during paving on Second
Avenue North near Union Street, in the vicinity of Printer's Alley, and
at the old Maxwell House Hotel.[10]

In the mid-nineteenth century, houses along North Market Street
and businesses overlooking the Public Square emptied their sewers
into large natural fissures in the bedrock discovered while excavating

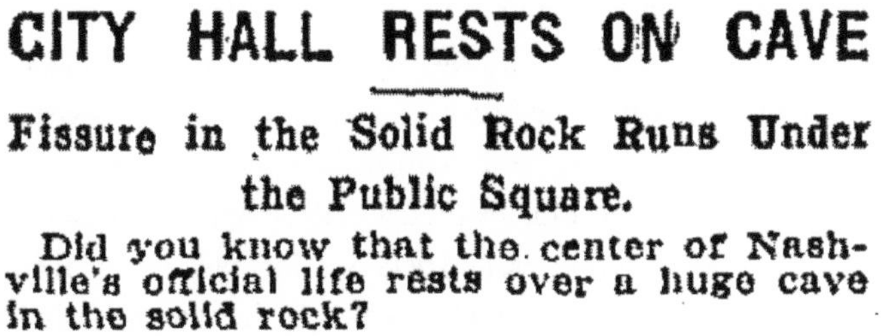

CITY HALL RESTS ON CAVE

Fissure in the Solid Rock Runs Under the Public Square.

Did you know that the center of Nashville's official life rests over a huge cave in the solid rock?

FIGURE 2.2. November 17, 1909, headline from the *Nashville American*, leading a historic account of caves located beneath Public Square.

their foundations.[11] This same strategy was later adopted by the city when workers encountered a natural crevasse while laying sewer lines near Second and Union Streets. In 1909 a story in the *Nashville American* noted that "For about forty years sewage has been pouring into that cavity and there is not the slightest sign of its filling up."[12] Other historical accounts describe underground crevasses unearthed during construction southwest of Public Square, near where the First American Bank was eventually constructed.[13]

Details as to the layout of the downtown caverns vary widely in historical sources. Several accounts describe a grand subterranean network reminiscent of Kentucky's Mammoth Cave. During the mid-1800s the City Hotel, which backed up to the Cumberland River bluff on the east side of Public Square, reportedly hosted cock fights in an underlying natural grotto.[14] At around that same time, a long-haired man who lived in a cabin near the old Davidson County jail reportedly gave twenty-five cent candlelight tours of underground caverns said to run all the way beneath City Hall.[15]

By some accounts, a cave mouth was once present along the Cumberland River bluff at the foot of Union Street.[16] That opening was situated below the Enterprise Soap Works and described as fifty feet wide and ten to twelve feet high, large enough inside to accommodate lumber storage. According to an 1874 article in the *Republican Banner*, the riverbank entrance connected to a network of large, sandy-floored chambers lit by gas lights, with sitting areas, a ballroom, and a bar.[17]

It is a stumbling block in historical research that early newspaper accounts are often prone to sensationalism and hyperbole. There was little or no fact checking by media outlets in the late nineteenth and early twentieth centuries, and details, informants, or even entire stories might be created out of whole cloth. In the case of Nashville's downtown caverns, there is unfortunately no direct evidence confirming that a passable cave network, or even the opening beneath the soap works, are anything other than tall tales.

A more likely description of the cave mouth along the river is found in an 1878 report from the *Daily American*, which describes an attempted exploration by participants from a meeting of the American Scientific Association.[18] The scientists, carrying with them their "necessary implements and instruments for a thorough scientific exploration," and accompanied by several hundred lookers-on, first visited a possible entrance on the bluff near what is today Bank Street. That opening was filled with refuse, and after twenty feet ended in a water-filled passage they were unable to traverse. They next inspected a small opening beneath the suspension bridge, which proved to be a narrow, dead-end passage. Today both those locations are situated below the Gay Street Connector and sealed behind a large stone retaining wall.

An examination of the local geology further reveals the suspect nature of the elaborate caves described in early newspaper reports. The sedimentary bedrock underlying downtown Nashville is composed of Ordovician-age Bigby Cannon limestone, formed between about 440 and 480 million years ago.[19] The particular structure of that stone does not weather in a manner that typically results in the formation of horizontal cave networks. According to Tennessee's state geologist Ron Zurawski, groundwater penetration and weathering of Bigby Cannon limestone primarily takes place along vertical, rather than horizontal joints. This results in the formation of

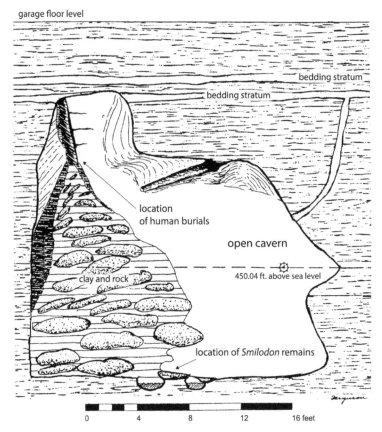

garage floor level

bedding stratum

bedding stratum

location
of human burials

open cavern

450.04 ft. above sea level

clay and rock

location of *Smilodon* remains

0   4   8   12   16 feet

FIGURE 2.3. The vertical profile of the First American Cave site in August 1971, adapted from a field sketch by Bob Ferguson. Image courtesy of the Tennessee Division of Archaeology.

crevasses called cutters, which extend down from the surface. Cutters in Bigby Cannon limestone can measure up to about forty feet deep and twenty-five feet wide at their tops, and may create long, intersecting channels. As they form, the cutters are filled from the top with a mixture of clay and weathered stone fragments. Over time, groundwater movement can flush out this fill material, leaving behind open areas; however, because they are connected to the surface they will continue to accumulate new fill over time.

This geologic picture fits well with the small portion of the cave observed at the First American Bank in 1971 (Figure 2.3). That is, it was the remnant of a cutter in the bedrock that by the last ice age had been at least partially flushed of its original fill material. The location of the original opening remains unknown, and it is not clear if the sabertooth cave connected to any of the other chasms described historically in the area. Regardless, any openings to the surface seem to have been closed off by at least the mid-1800s.

Just two historical accounts of crevasses near Public Square note discoveries of bones or fossils. In 1876 the *Daily American* describes that workers excavating building foundations on Union Street encountered a sinkhole containing "a lot of dog bones" which were "lugged home as great prizes."[20] Several years later, the *Nashville American* recounted stories of a cave beneath Public Square containing "the half-imbedded remains of aquatics, the bones of fishes, and other evidence of extinct animal existence."[21] Unfortunately, no further details are given as to what that "other evidence" may have been.

Sabertooth Cats in Nashville and Beyond

Thankfully, the 1971 First American bank excavations resulted in much more specific information on Nashville's deep past. Paleontologist John Guilday of the Carnegie Museum of Natural History in Pittsburgh conducted a formal examination of the bones recovered from the First American Bank site, and in 1977 he published the first and only account of those remains.[22] According to Guilday's inventory, more than one thousand animal bones and bone fragments, representing over thirty separate vertebrate species, were recovered from the cave. Remains from the upper levels of the deposit, which contained the human burials, also included animals such as snakes, opossum, skunk, shrew, rabbits, mice, and raccoons. The lower portion of the cave included the sabertooth cat remains and bones of

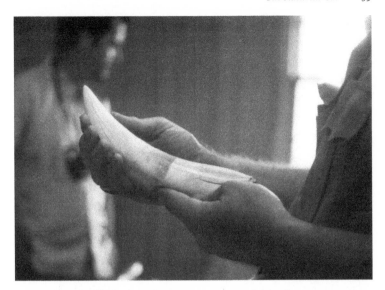

FIGURE 2.4. Bob Ferguson examines the sabertooth canine found at the First American Cave site on August 12, 1971. Photograph by Les Leverett.

other extinct mammals such as long-nosed peccary, musk ox, and the partial skeleton of a young horse. Nearly two-thirds of the animal bones recovered from the site, including those of domestic hogs, a bobcat, the tooth of a young mastodon, and more of the horse skeleton, came from areas that had been disturbed by heavy machinery, or were found in the construction dump.

Excavations recovered a total of 119 bones and bone fragments belonging to the sabertooth cat, of which only a quarter were found still within the cave. Those remains included portions of all four limbs, the ribs, vertebrae, cranium, and the right upper canine (Figure 2.4). Many of the sabertooth bones had been badly fractured by heavy machinery, and most of the jaw, including the left canine, were never recovered.

Sabertooth cats are immediately recognizable thanks to their oversized, somewhat curved upper canines like the one found that day in Nashville. Although often called "sabertooth tigers" they are not closely related to living tigers or other big cats. A recent study of ancient DNA shows that the sabertooth lineage last shared a common ancestor with modern cats around 20 million years ago.[23]

While many species of long-fanged felids have roamed the earth, just two biological genera of sabertooth inhabited the Americas at the end of the last ice age.[24] The smaller of these were the scimitar cats (genus *Homotherium*), which were found throughout much of the world beginning about four million years ago. The second, more robust group, the genus *Smilodon*, had longer and larger teeth, and were indigenous only to the Americas.[25] Both *Homotherium* and *Smilodon* became extinct around 12,000 years ago, at the end of the Pleistocene epoch.

Two species of *Smilodon* were present in the Western Hemisphere up until the end of the last ice age. *Smilodon populator*, the larger of the two, weighed up to around 800 pounds and appears to have lived only in South America. Based on size measurements, the skeletal material from the First American Bank belongs instead to *Smilodon fatalis*. These short-tailed cats stood over three feet tall, weighed up to about 620 pounds, and appear in the fossil record from Canada south to Chile.[26] Prior to that day in 1971, only a single *Smilodon* fossil had ever been identified in Tennessee, found in 1921 in a cave in Hawkins County.[27]

The bank funded radiocarbon dating of two samples extracted from the sabertooth bones, which returned ages of around 8700 BC and 9600 BC. These results are somewhat suspect, in that the more recent portion of that range is some 2,000 years younger than any other dated *Smilodon fatalis* specimens.[28] If the dates are correct, the Nashville sabertooth is the geologically youngest *Smilodon* known, and may have been one of the last of its kind living on Earth.

Nashville has our own resident expert on sabertooth teeth. Larisa DeSantis is a paleontologist and professor in Vanderbilt's Departments of Biological Science and Earth and Environmental Sciences. She founded and directs the DeSantis DREAM Lab (Dietary Reconstructions and Ecological Assessments of Mammals) at Vanderbilt, and is part of the collaborative SABER Project (Stable Isotopes, Anatomy, Behavior, Ecology, and Radiometric Dating). Several times over the past decade DeSantis has lent us her expertise and use of her lab equipment for our various research projects, none of which, we're sorry to say, have cool acronyms.

DeSantis grew up in Los Angeles and was drawn to paleontology following childhood visits to Rancho La Brea, the famous La Brea Tar Pits site in Los Angeles, California. For some 50,000 years around the end of the last ice age and still today, natural asphalt seeps at La Brea acted as a trap for various herbivore species and the predators that their struggles attracted, and the site has produced the largest collection of sabertooth cat fossils anywhere on earth. Today DeSantis uses dental molds, high-powered microscopes, and isotope analysis to examine the chemical composition, minute wear patterns, and breakage on teeth of both living and extinct carnivores. That data allows DeSantis and her colleagues to better understand the diets of now-extinct animals during the last few weeks of their lives, and to reconstruct the ancient ecosystems in which those animals lived.

The chemical composition of tooth enamel reflects the average diet of an animal. In the case of predators, stable carbon isotopes from the teeth also show which plants their prey consumed, and allow DeSantis to determine whether those plants, and therefore the prey animals themselves, were native to open grasslands or forest canopy environments. Her results show that *Smilodon* and the other large cats from La Brea specialized in hunting within both canopied forests and shrubland environments.[29]

Smilodon fatalis teeth from the La Brea site exhibit microwear similar to modern African lions, revealing a generalized diet that included both flesh and bone.[30] However, those specimens lack the

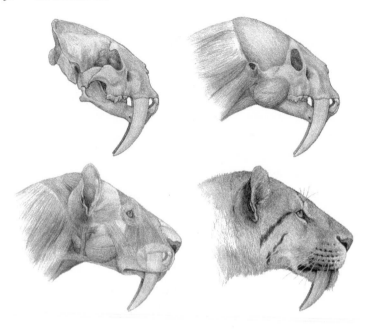

FIGURE 2.5. Reconstruction of the head of a Smilodon by paleoartist Mauricio Antón.

dramatic pitting associated with carcass consumption found among modern hyenas. These data show that even as extinction approached at the end of the Pleistocene, sabertooth cats were not suffering from critical food shortages that drove them to fully consume or scavenge carcasses.[31] The stability of their food source is also evidenced by a general absence of nutritional stress in the skeletal remains from *Smilodon* and other late-Pleistocene mammals at La Brea.[32]

Studies of tooth breakage on fossils from Rancho La Brea show that sabertooth cats and other extinct carnivores at that site all fractured their canine teeth more frequently than living carnivores such as wolves, coyotes, and lions.[33] However, while the overall tooth breakage patterns for carnivores at La Brea are higher than in living animals, sabertooth cats from that site suffered less canine breakage than Pleistocene dire wolfs, American lions, or coyotes, all of which have conical, more proportional fangs.[34] This suggests that *Smilodons* evolved a hunting strategy to specifically avoid tooth injuries. Older interpretations of sabertooth cat behavior focus on their taking large prey like bison and mammoth by using their oversize canines to attack and bring down those animals. However, sabertooth skulls and jaws are poorly suited to withstand the forces created by struggles of large, unrestrained prey (Figure 2.5).

The modern picture of sabertooth hunting is that of an ambush predator that surprised and overpowered their prey. After bringing down and restraining an animal with a combination of body weight and powerful forelimbs, the cat would then use its fangs to administer the coup de grâce in what is called a "canine-shear bite." This technique used the well-developed neck muscles and lower jaw in sequence, driving their large incisors into the restrained prey's throat, and quickly bringing about death as a result of blood loss.

Smilodon are among the various species of ice age megafauna that went extinct in North America at the end of the Pleistocene. Other notable large-bodied mammals that disappeared around the same time include the mastodon, mammoth, American lion, and giant ground sloth. Ultimately the extinction of sabertooth cats was likely a result of changing late ice age environments and the extinction of their prey, the cause of which is still debated. Radiocarbon data suggest that the sabertooth cats persisted in North America for several millennia after the arrival of the First Americans. It is possible that competition from human hunters contributed to sabertooth extinction, although there is not yet any conclusive archaeological evidence of human interaction with these predators. No *Smilodon* skeletons or even individual bones have been found at any Paleoindian period sites, and there is not yet unambiguous proof that the First Americans ever hunted, or were hunted by, sabertooth cats.

Interpreting the First American Cave: Exhibits and Revisits

Following the 1971 excavations, all of the bones from the First American Bank site were stored at Vanderbilt University's Department of Anthropology, where they were cleaned and catalogued. After building construction was completed, the Southeastern Indian Antiquities Survey organized a display for the Bank lobby. Beneath a wall-mounted timeline, two standard-issue glass museum display cases presented a selection of bones. One exhibited remains of peccary and of the sabertooth cat, including several jaw fragments and the fang. These were displayed alongside a replica cast of a complete *Smilodon* skull, made after an original recovered at Rancho La Brea. The second case displayed an assortment of smaller animal remains, and portions of at least two human skeletons from the site.

The bank exhibit was later reorganized, perhaps in part to address concerns regarding public exhibition of Native American skeletons. Neither the human bones nor the iconic fang were present in the new display. In 1990, First American National Bank was absorbed by AmSouth Bancorporation, and the downtown tower became that organization's Tennessee headquarters. John Dowd, one of the SIAS members who participated in the 1971 excavations and who recorded the cave site with the Division of Archaeology, recalls that around this time he was contacted by lawyers from AmSouth who were attempting to locate all of First American's assets.[35] They were specifically interested in determining the location of the materials from the cave, and particularly the sabertooth fang. Dowd could unfortunately provide no leads. Rumors at the time suggested the tooth had been sent to the Smithsonian, although that institution has no record of such a transfer.

After the bank building was completed in 1974, the cave remnants sat mostly forgotten and the Nashville sabertooth slipped out of the public consciousness for nearly two decades. In 1997, the *Smilodon*

FIGURE 2.6. The original Nashville Predator's logo, used during the 1998-99 to 2010-11 hockey seasons. The Nashville Predators name and primary logo are registered trademarks of the NHL Team. ©NHL 2020. All rights reserved. Used with permission.

was reintroduced to Nashville via an unexpected intermediary: the National Hockey League. In June of that year, the NHL granted a franchise expansion for Nashville to Leipold Hockey Holdings, officially bringing professional hockey to Music City. Three months later, the organization held a press conference at the former First American Bank building to unveil the team's logo: the snarling profile of a sabertooth cat (Figure 2.6).

Although the logo was decided, the team name was still to be determined. After the original suggestion of "Edge" was rejected by the NHL, the organization market-tested options including "Fury," "Ice Tigers" (later changed to just "Tigers"), and the most popular choice in public polling, "Predators."[36] The Predators name was officially announced on November 13, 1997.

In 2008, two years after the purchase of AmSouth by Regions Financial Corporation, Aaron reached out to the Nashville headquarters of Regions Bank regarding the status of the cave site and the possibility of performing a re-inspection. Neither the bank employees nor the

FIGURE 2.7. Tennessee Division of Archaeology personnel inspect the First American Cave in 2008. The cave remnants extend approximately eight feet beneath the concrete bank foundation to the right of the frame. Photograph by Aaron Deter-Wolf.

staff of the building management company were aware that a portion of the cave still existed, although several had heard rumors of underground Confederate escape tunnels that allegedly ran beneath the building, connecting the riverbank to the State Capitol.

In August of that year, Aaron and three colleagues from the Division of Archaeology reentered the First American Cave (Figure 2.7).[37] In the bottom of the bank's parking garage they were let through a large steel hatch, beneath which was a metal ladder bolted to the concrete foundation. Several floodlights attached to the same wall illuminated a solid face of bedrock, six feet away. The ladder descended about twenty feet to the bottom of the foundation, which partially vaults above a low opening measuring only about five feet tall by fifteen feet square. This is the final remnant of the sabertooth cave, its floor and walls made up of a muddy reddish-brown sediment. There are no visible passages leading from the space.

The remaining cave floor was wet from moisture moving through the surrounding bedrock, and small pools of standing water and pieces of rusted metal from the building substructure were scattered across the muddy surface. The archaeologists collected a sample of cave soils, which were later examined at the Division of Archaeology. Those sediments contained fragments of natural limestone, along with a small number of tiny marine fossils originating in the surrounding bedrock. No bones or artifacts were present.

After being in the space beneath the bank and looking back over the original excavation reports, Aaron determined that the sabertooth skeleton was probably recovered several feet above the existing cave floor. This means any remaining cave deposits beneath the bank predate that animal, as well as human occupation in Tennessee. For this reason, the surviving remnants of the First American Cave are now considered a paleontological site rather than an archaeological one.

The bank building was renamed the UBS Tower in 2013, after the banking giant who became the new principal tenant, and three years later it was announced that the bones from the bank lobby had been transferred to the Nashville Predators organization for exhibition in the downtown hockey arena.[38] Today those remains, along with an interpretive panel formerly located in the AmSouth/Regions lobby, are installed in a display case in the Guest Services area of the arena concourse. Beneath the case, a blue and gold banner reads "Ice Age to Ice Hockey." The cast of the La Brea *Smilodon* skull remains the exhibit centerpiece, surrounded by several dozen animal bones. Small markers beside the bones identify them by species according to text in the panel. The case includes a handful of the actual sabertooth remains, including several teeth, and long bone and jaw fragments.

The bones on display in the arena represent less than a quarter of the total sabertooth remains inventoried by Guilday, and an even smaller percentage of the complete collection from the site. Unfortunately, we have not been able to locate the remainder of the materials Ferguson and the SIAS excavated from the First American Cave. It is possible that those fossils are curated at Vanderbilt's Department of Anthropology along with the human remains from the site, although we have not been able to obtain any confirmation of their status. The whereabouts of the iconic fang remain unknown.

With permission of the Predators organization, DeSantis hopes in the future to conduct further scientific studies on the Nashville *Smilodon* remains. The surviving teeth now on display in the hockey arena would allow a study of microwear patterns, examination of the dental isotopes, and possibly new radiocarbon dates, all of which might reveal important new details about the last days of Nashville's most famous ice age predator. More than 10,000 years since its death, and almost a half-century after its discovery, the story of the Nashville sabertooth and what it can tell us about ancient Nashville is not yet complete.

CHAPTER 3

Furry Elephants and the First Nashvillians

One of the first things visitors see on entering the Tennessee State Museum's permanent exhibit, titled "The First Peoples," is the massive lower jaw of an ice age elephant. That fossil, found in the Harpeth River in western Davidson County, measures thirty-five inches long and sports four rugged teeth, each the size of a football (Figure 3.1). Both the jawbone and the tip of a fossilized ivory tusk rest in front of a wall-size painting in which four muscular Native American men in loincloths surround a fur-covered elephant. The animal is in distress, trapped in a muddy bog as the hunters stab at it with stone-tipped spears. This vignette tells the commonly accepted story of how the First American occupants of the Cumberland River valley procured their dinners around 13,000 years ago, during the Paleoindian period.

The extinction of mastodons, sabertooth cats, and other ice age megafauna in the Americas follows shortly on the heels of the first people arriving in the Western Hemisphere. The specific timing of the journey by the First Americans and the routes that they traveled remain the topic of public interest and ongoing archaeological research. While new details on the peopling of the Americas continue to emerge, the prevailing archaeological consensus is that the first humans to arrive in North America did so around 14,000 to 15,000

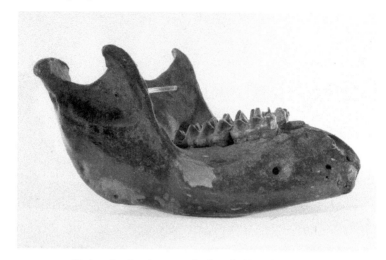

FIGURE 3.1. The jaw of an American mastodon from the Harpeth River, on display at the Tennessee State Museum. The jaw measures 14.5 inches tall by 35 inches long. Image courtesy of the Tennessee State Museum–Tennessee Historical Society.

years ago following a multi-generational journey across Beringia, the now-submerged landmass that connected Siberia and Alaska.

The movement of people into the New World at the end of the Pleistocene epoch was not a one-time event. Other later, and possibly earlier, journeys across Beringia and along the Pacific coast brought groups of people into the Americas over a period of thousands of years. This was also not a one-way trip, and by about 12,000 years ago some First American communities were migrating north back through the Ice Free Corridor and into Alaska.[1]

Several highly publicized studies over the last decade have suggested much earlier dates for the presence of humans in the Americas, and proposed alternative routes of travel, including along the Atlantic ice sheets from Europe. Those suggestions have sparked the public imagination and led to much archaeological debate. However, no evidence presented to date has overturned the decades of linguistic, genetic, and artifact studies that inform the modern archaeological understanding of the arrival of the First Americans.

FIGURE 3.2. Drawing showing (left to right) a mammoth, a mastodon, and a very lucky—or unlucky—First American hunter. After James X. Corgan and Emmanuel Breitburg, *Tennessee's Prehistoric Vertebrates*, Tennessee Division of Geology Bulletin 84 (Nashville: State of Tennessee Department of Environment and Conservation, 1996), fig. 22.

Radiocarbon data is scarce for late ice age archaeological sites in Middle Tennessee, and we do not know precisely when the First Americans first reached the Cumberland River valley. We do know that by about 13,000 years ago the people who called the area home lived in a very different environment than is found in modern Nashville, and one that included a variety of now-extinct large animal species. The story of how these people interacted with Pleistocene megafauna, and particularly with ice age elephants, has been one of ongoing scientific discovery, and sometimes overturned conclusions.

Ice Age Elephants

Mastodons and mammoths are not the same creatures, although they look similar enough that we sometimes forget they are two separate species (Figure 3.2). While both are members of the biological order Proboscidea, the Columbian mammoths that once roamed the American Southeast belong to the genus *Mammuthus* in the family Elephantidae, as do modern living elephants. American mastodons on the other hand belong in the genus *Mammut*, part of the now-extinct family Mammutidae. Although they are first cousins, metaphorically speaking, mammoths and modern elephants are more closely related to each other than either are to mastodons.

From a physical perspective, mammoths are larger than mastodons, with more dramatically curved tusks, taller skulls, and fatty humps on their backs—picture of course the character Manny from the *Ice Age* movies. When looking at the skeletal remains of these animals, the most distinctive difference between mammoths and mastodons is found in their teeth, and consequently their diets. Mammoths were grazers, and their wide molars were covered in parallel ridges adapted to grinding up grassy vegetation. Mastodons, on the other hand, were browsers. Studies of microscopic tooth wear and of mastodon stomach contents preserved in wet environments show that they foraged in mixed woodland settings.[2] This diet is reflected in the shape of mastodon molars, which as seen in Figure 3.1, have high, cone-shaped cusps that are well suited for crushing leaves, twigs, and branches. Over time the individual cusps would wear down at their peaks, resulting in a cup-shaped appearance. These dental protrusions lent the animals their name, from the Greek *mastos* + *odont* ("breast tooth"), and gave rise to eighteenth-century debates as to if mastodons—then known as the *American incognitum*—were herbivores or carnivores.[3]

There have been around eighty recorded discoveries of ice age elephants in Tennessee over the past two centuries.[4] The details of many of these encounters are difficult to establish, as they have only been reported second- or third-hand.[5] Some specimens, like Shumate's "grand Monster Tennessean" described in Chapter 1, and pieces from the collection of the former Nashville Children's Museum, have been entirely lost. Despite these issues, we know that about 90 percent of the reliably identified ice age elephant remains from Tennessee are mastodon rather than mammoth. The largest concentration of mastodon remains in the state are found in Davidson and Williamson Counties, where bones have been recovered from more than twenty sites, including stream beds, crevasses, historic wells, and stone quarries. During the last ice age, Nashville was apparently a good place to be a mastodon.

Dutch-born geologist and paleontologist Gerard Troost moved to Nashville in 1828, bringing with him an extensive personal collection of minerals, fossils, and Native American artifacts.[6] To those he added the holdings of the former Nashville Museum, all of which he exhibited to the public in his Nashville Museum of Natural History.[7] In 1831 Troost was appointed Tennessee's first state geologist, mineralogist, and assayer. At that time Tennessee's geological history was literally a blank slate: there had been no formal studies, nor were there any official state maps. Troost traveled extensively, documenting the state's geology and soils, while also noting details of the fossil record and expanding his personal collection. In 1834 and 1835, he reported discoveries of mastodon remains at two sites in Williamson County, one along the upper Harpeth River in the vicinity of College Grove, and a second within a wet-weather creek near the Liberty Meeting House in Bellevue.[8] At the second location, Troost noted that the head of the animal's femur extended above the ground and was used by locals as a step to cross the creek when it contained water.[9]

Discoveries of other ice age elephants in Nashville continued throughout the late nineteenth century. On July 21, 1887, the *Daily American* reported a remarkable discovery by workers digging a well near Sulphur Dell, between what is today First Tennessee Park and Bicentennial Mall.[10] At a depth of about twenty-seven feet, diggers encountered an obstruction, which they assumed to be a buried log. "Without further ado, pickaxes were brought into play, and the log cut in pieces and thrown out with the soil," the story reports. It was only later that several of these pieces, reportedly measuring about nine inches in diameter, found their way to the state geologist and were identified as tusk fragments from a mastodon or mammoth.

New discoveries of mastodon remains in Middle Tennessee continue today as a result of construction, exploration, and examinations of old collections. Alan Brown, director of the Earth Experience – the Middle Tennessee Museum of Natural History in Murfreesboro, tells us that Tennessee citizens have brought close to a dozen mastodon specimens into the museum over the past decade. In 2016, our contacts in the caver community shared with us a submerged cave site in Middle Tennessee that contained both mastodon and mammoth remains. Based on the local geology, it appears those animals likely fell into a sinkhole extending below the water table, and their bones subsequently washed along an underground stream passage through the bedrock.

The Coats-Hines Site

Of the many mastodon sites in Middle Tennessee, only one has been formally excavated and the subject of modern scientific analysis. The Coats-Hines site is located in Brentwood, just five miles from where Troost recorded mastodon remains near the Liberty Meeting House. Excavations between 1977 and 2012 produced some remarkable data on ice age Middle Tennessee, while also serving as a reminder to archaeologists that it's important to retest and reevaluate our hypotheses.

In 1977, landscaping work at the Crockett Springs Golf Course in Brentwood uncovered several large bones within in a stream channel. Emanuel Breitburg, then a zooarchaeologist at the Tennessee Division of Archaeology, was notified of the find. Breitburg and other Division staff performed a short salvage excavation, recovering the partial skeleton of an adult female mastodon.

No further investigations took place at the site until the spring of 1994, when work began on a new 1,100-acre residential development just downstream from the golf course. That year Breitburg

FIGURE 3.3. Excavations at the Coats-Hines site in 1994. The large bones throughout the photograph are mastodon remains, situated approximately eight feet below ground surface. Photograph courtesy of the Tennessee Division of Archaeology.

and archaeologist John Broster, one of the foremost researchers on Paleoindian sites in Tennessee, examined the drainage and discovered more large bones. These included a vertebra, ribs, and a tusk, all eroding out of the base of the streambank less than one hundred feet away from the 1977 finds.[11] Breitburg and Broster contacted the developer, the Hines corporation out of Houston, Texas, and asked for permission to further investigate the area. Since that portion of the property was not slated for immediate construction, the Division of Archaeology was allowed to conduct an excavation.

The 1994 effort uncovered a variety of well-preserved animal bones between about six and nine feet below ground surface, situated within and beneath what appeared to be a layer of dark gray clay (Figure 3.3).[12] Those remains included deer, muskrat, canid (a general term that includes dog, coyote, or wolf), turtle, and a young male mastodon. The skeleton of the elephant was incomplete, and the bones were not in anatomical position. Based on the local terrain and the soils surrounding the bones, the archaeologists proposed that the area had once been a shallow pond, perhaps formed by a blockage along the stream drainage. The animal remains appeared to be those of creatures who had died at this watering hole.

The excavations also recovered several possible human-made artifacts from around the animal bones and from within bulk soil samples. In the initial 1995 publication of the discovery in *Tennessee Conservationist* magazine, excavators described finding several dozen pieces of flint within the same dark gray clay soil that contained the bones.[13] Some of those appeared to be stone tools, while others seemed to be flakes created by making or sharpening stone implements. With the discovery of these artifacts, the area was officially designated an archaeological site, rather than a paleontological one, and was given the name Coats-Hines after the developer (Hines) and long-time Division of Archaeology employee Patricia Coats. While the data suggested both humans and ice age animals were present on the landscape when the site formed, there was not yet evidence to directly connect the two.

Back at the Division of Archaeology lab, Breitburg and Broster used a microscope to examine the remains of the mastodon and identified sets of lines and gouges on the surface of two bones: a vertebrae (spine) and also a humerus (the upper leg bone). Some of these marks appeared to be V-shaped in profile, suggesting they were created by cutting action with stone tools, as opposed to natural processes such as animal gnawing. There had been no prior evidence of humans hunting or butchering megafauna in Tennessee, and very few such sites were known in eastern North America. Suddenly, the Coats-Hines site appeared to be hugely important for understanding the culture and history of the First Americans. It was, by all appearances, Tennessee's first barbeque.

2 in

FIGURE 3.4. Fluted Paleoindian period spear points from Davidson County. Image courtesy of the Tennessee State Museum.

First American Tools and Hunting Practices

The diets of the First Americans have fascinated paleontologists, geologists, archaeologists, zoologists, and the public ever since the first discovery of stone tools alongside ice age megafauna. During the early twentieth century, finds of Paleoindian period tools associated with the bones of mammoth and other megafauna at sites like Blackwater Draw, near Clovis, New Mexico, helped establish a perception of the First Americans as peerless big-game hunters. The distinctive artifacts found at these sites, finely worked stone points that have a channel flake (known as a flute to archaeologists) removed from the base on one or both faces, came to be synonymous with the earliest human culture in the Americas (Figure 3.4). We don't know exactly why the First Americans fluted their spear points, although one recent study suggests that the removal of that flake makes the base of the point better able to absorb the shock of colliding with hard objects, such as the bones of ice age elephants.[14]

The earliest fluted tools are known as Clovis points, named after the town near Blackwater Draw, and are perhaps the first great American invention. Until recently, no comparable fluted stone tools were known from any other region on earth, including northeastern Siberia, where decades of archaeological speculation and recent DNA analysis show the ancestors of the First Americans originated.[15] Instead, fluted points discovered from dated archaeological contexts in Alaska appear to be younger than those found at sites below the glacial sheets, suggesting that the technology evolved in temperate regions of what is now the continental United States and then was carried back north, as opposed to being developed in Siberia or Beringia and then moving south. In 2020, a new archaeological study revealed the presence of fluted point technology in the southern Arabian Peninsula at sites dated to around 6000 BC. Those points post-date the North American technology by around 5,000 years, and show a fascinating case of independent re-invention.[16]

Research by the team behind the Paleoindian Database of the Americas, helmed by University of Tennessee Knoxville professor David G. Anderson, has allowed them to map the distributions of all the American fluted points discovered north of the Rio Grande. Those data show that there are significantly more fluted points east of the Mississippi than in the American Southwest.[17] Moreover, in terms of overall number of artifacts, the Tennessee and Cumberland River valleys seem to be home to the densest concentration of fluted points in North America.[18] This suggests that there were more people present on the landscape and making fluted points in the Cumberland River valley during the Paleoindian period than in nearly any other region in North America.

Unfortunately, intact archaeological sites dating to the late Pleistocene and early Holocene in Middle Tennessee remain mostly elusive, and artifact preservation from this period is limited almost entirely to stone tools. While we know that the First Americans were present in Tennessee, that knowledge is based primarily on artifacts from private collections rather than controlled archaeological excavations. This limits our ability to understand the overall culture, social organization, and diets of Nashville's earliest occupants, and so instead we must rely largely on data excavated from sites elsewhere in the American Southeast.

The timing of the arrival of the First Americans relative to the final disappearance of mastodons and other North American megafauna, along with discoveries at sites like Blackwater Draw, were used in the 1960s to suggest that human hunting was partially or wholly responsible for megafaunal extinctions.[19] That idea came to be known as the Overkill Hypothesis, a model in which Paleoindian hunters were seen as super-predators, armed with deadly fluted spear points on a virgin landscape filled with large game species that did not recognize or fear humans. According to the Overkill Hypothesis, the megafauna's naiveté was their downfall, and humans quickly hunted those animals into oblivion.

During the second half of the twentieth century, scenes such as the one in the Tennessee State Museum, with groups of spear-wielding First Americans mobbing trapped elephants, became the default picture of Paleoindian subsistence. Popular understanding of First American lifeways focused on the idea that small, nomadic family bands constantly moved about the American landscape in pursuit of large herds of megafauna, which made up their primary food source. Despite the general appeal of this image and of the Overkill Hypothesis, actual archaeological data supporting these ideas was fairly sparse. When the Coats-Hines site was excavated in 1994, direct evidence of humans hunting or butchering mastodons was known from only a handful of sites in all of North America.

Nearly thirty years later, the archaeological evidence remains ephemeral. Fewer than twenty archaeological sites in North America present reliable evidence for human hunting of megafaunal mammals.[20] Within that sample, just five out of thirty-seven genera of extinct megafauna are represented: mammoths, mastodons, horses, camels, and gomphotheres, another elephant-like proboscidean.[21] Mastodons are present at just two of the agreed-upon megafauna sites, which do not, for reasons we'll soon learn, include Coats-Hines.

What this very limited evidence tells us about the diets of the First Americans is open for debate. The very small number of sites may indicate that Native Americans rarely hunted mastodons. The sample size might alternately be the result of poor bone preservation, a common issue at late Pleistocene archaeological sites. Anecdotally, the emerging archaeological consensus regarding megafaunal extinctions is a multifaceted one: The fossil record shows that the extinction of megafauna in the Americas began around 40,000 BC, long before the proven arrival of the First Americans. This process was a slow transition that coincides with, and is likely related to, gradual global climate shifts at the end of the last ice age. The combination of changing temperatures, shifting seasonal lengths, and resulting alterations to the environment would have profoundly impacted the food resources and reproductive success of large herbivores. The arrival of the First Americans and their hunting practices toward the end of this period undoubtedly contributed to the final disappearance of at least some species of megafauna, but was probably not the sole, or even the primary cause of those extinctions.

New Discoveries at Coats-Hines

Following the 1994 excavations at Coats-Hines, archaeologists with the Division of Archaeology continued to periodically examine the stream channel and further study materials recovered from the site. Radiocarbon samples collected during the 1994 excavations returned a wide range of dates, from as early as 29,800 BC to as recent as 5400 BC. These dates are somewhat problematic: there is no widely accepted evidence for human presence in the Americas at the upper end of that range, while the more recent period falls over five thousand years after the major megafaunal extinctions. Only one sample, run on sediment from beneath the mastodon rib, returned a date of about 12,000 BC and so seemed to generally fit with the timeline of First American occupations in Tennessee. Further lab work sifting through soil samples from the site also recovered two small bone fragments identified as a possible spear point and a pressure flaker, an artifact used for making and sharpening stone tools.[22] Finally, in 1995 more large, extremely fragmentary bones of a possible third mastodon were discovered eroding further downstream in the same drainage.

In 2008 one of Tanya's undergraduate students at MTSU, Jesse Tune, spent the summer interning with Aaron at the Division of Archaeology. While none of us could know it at the time, Tune would come to play a central role in the story of the Coats-Hines site. At that time very few archaeologists other than staff at the Division of Archaeology were researching the Paleoindian period in Tennessee, and the data on most of those sites were not widely available. Tune, a Middle Tennessee native, became intrigued by differences between the modern environment and ecosystems and those of the late Pleistocene, and the adaptations and strategies the First Americans developed to live and thrive in late ice age conditions. He went on to earn his PhD in anthropology, along the way conducting research on Coats-Hines and a number of other Tennessee sites and artifact collections. That work has included projects applying new research strategies and technologies to the study of the earliest inhabitants of North America and has resulted in some surprising finds along the way. As he told us, "sometimes you discover you're not working on the same puzzle you thought you were."

During his 2008 internship, Tune helped catalog Paleoindian period artifacts from across the state and assisted with site inspections. That summer he and Aaron revisited the drainage at Coats-Hines and recovered several stone tools within the streambed. Those were not artifact types that could be assigned a specific age based on their shape, making them "non-diagnostic" in archaeological parlance. They were also not in their original context, having washed into the stream from an unknown location. The drainage at Coats-Hines runs through a low-lying basin flanked on three sides by elevated terrain that now holds residential cul-de-sacs. When those areas were being cleared for construction in the 1990s, archaeologists recorded several small scatters of stone tools less than a foot below surface in bulldozer cuts. Those included artifacts from both the Archaic and Woodland periods, and based on their position overlooking the wet-weather stream, were probably the remains of small, temporary hunting encampments. While it was intriguing to think that the stone tools found in the streambed in 2008 might be from Coats-Hines, it was more likely that they eroded from the more recent, shallowly buried sites.

Nevertheless, the 2008 discoveries brought the Coats-Hines site to our attention and raised the possibility that it still contained intact archaeological deposits. We felt strongly that if this site was truly a 13,000-year-old mastodon butchering camp, its uniqueness and importance needed to be acknowledged. In the world of cultural resources and historic preservation, the gold standard is to have such sites listed on the National Register of Historic Places, the "official list of the Nation's historic places worthy of preservation" maintained by the National Park Service. The National Register includes over two thousand historic properties, buildings, districts, and archaeological sites from Tennessee, and more than ninety-five thousand listings nationwide. The eligibility of an archaeological site for inclusion on the National Register depends on its age, significance, and integrity: it must be at least fifty years old, be associated with important events, activities, developments, or individuals, or have the potential to yield significant information about the past through controlled archeological investigation.

FIGURE 3.5. MTSU anthropology students collect soil samples during excavations at the Coats-Hines site in 2010. Photograph by Aaron Deter-Wolf.

We believed the significance of the Coats-Hines site lay not just in the presence of ice age animal bones, but also in what those remains might reveal about the lives of the First Americans. The age of approximately 12,000 BC, if correct, also made Coats-Hines the oldest dated archaeological site in Tennessee, a status we felt was worth acknowledging and promoting. As of 2010 the site had been incorporated into a suburban backyard, and it was not clear if any portion remained intact and so would meet the criteria for listing on the National Register. The only way to find out was to dig a big hole, in a controlled and scientific manner, of course.

That is how in October 2010, we came to find ourselves, along with Tune, Broster, and six undergraduate anthropology students from MTSU, deep in a trench searching for 12,000-year-old bones and stone tools (Figure 3.5). When we approached the property owners for permission to excavate, they were interested despite not having previously known what their backyard contained. It's one thing for someone to grant permission to dig a forty-five-foot-long, twelve-foot-deep hole in their backyard; it's another for them to remain gracious during the process. We could not have asked for better hosts.

As the hole grew deeper and deeper, with no evidence of archaeological materials in sight, our expectations began to drop. Then, about nine feet below ground surface, we encountered bones. After days of painstaking troweling and documentation, we closed up the excavation and headed back to the Division of Archaeology to consider what we'd found. Ultimately we recovered over 1,500 pieces of animal bone, although almost all of it was fragmentary and smaller than ¼-inch. Even if any of those bone bits were formerly part of a mastodon leg, vertebra, or any one of the more than three hundred bones in an elephant's body, there was no way to visually identify them as such given their size.

We ran four radiocarbon dates on samples collected in the vicinity of the recovered bones. As with the results from the 1994 excavations, our samples returned an extremely wide age range of between about 31,600 BC and AD 31. Again, just one sample, dated to approximately 12,500 BC, fell within the established range for First American occupations. Our excavations also recovered possible stone artifacts, including two potential blade fragments and more small flakes. All of those stones came from bulk soil samples rather than in direct association with animal bones, and while none exhibited physical attributes definitively indicating they were human-made, we believed that the collection of artifacts previously identified at the site provided appropriate context for classifying them as cultural remains rather than natural stone breakage.

While the radiocarbon dates were not ideal, the site could now be shown to contain more buried animal remains and possible stone tools. If properly excavated, these data might provide important information on the past environment and on First American adaptations and technologies. Using the results of the 2010 testing, the Coats-Hines site was nominated for inclusion in the National Register of Historic Places. Following a review of the nomination by both Tennessee's State Review Board and the National Park Service Keeper of the Register, the site was listed on the National Register in July 2011.

Since being listed on the National Register, the Coats-Hines site has become a part of the Tennessee Social Studies curriculum standards. During their study of Tennessee history, fifth graders learn to "Identify the cultures of the major indigenous settlements in Tennessee."[23] For the Paleoindian period, unfortunately misidentified in the curriculum as just the "Paleo," the standards specify inclusion of the Coats-Hines site. There are no official materials supporting this portion of the curriculum, leaving Tennessee's teachers to determine on their own what aspects of the site are most important for interpreting the lives of the First Americans. For obvious reasons, lessons about the Paleoindian period therefore include a strong focus on mastodon hunting at Coats-Hines. However, additional research has shown this story to be incorrect.

The scientific process can, and should, include using new methods, technologies, and lines of evidence to test and retest hypotheses. Doing so may reveal new information that in some cases can bolster and help refine earlier conclusions, while in other instances it may turn those theories on their heads. In 2012, Tune returned to Coats-Hines along with an archaeological crew from Texas A&M University's Center for the Study of the First Americans to conduct new excavations. With the benefit of a large budget and crew, that project was able to expose and examine around 460 square feet of the site, far more than had been previously investigated. They collected more finely controlled data to evaluate the site chronology and geological setting, and in the process revealed new, unexpected information.

The 2012 excavation confirmed that additional ice age animal remains were buried along the stream drainage. Larisa DeSantis, the vertebrate paleontologist from Vanderbilt we talked to in Chapter 2, examined the recovered animal remains and determined that more than 95 percent of the identifiable bones belonged to painted turtle.[24] Fragmentary remains of mastodon, deer, and horse were also identified, as well as giant ground sloth. None of these remains showed evidence of human modification or were found in association with artifacts.

Prior excavations at Coats-Hines did not include detailed studies of the local geomorphology, and so the landform history and geologic processes that created the site had not been fully delineated. The Texas A&M project revealed that the dark gray clay surrounding the buried animal remains at Coats-Hines was not a single soil deposit, but instead was laid down by a series of sporadic, powerful water pulses. The soils around the bones were therefore not formed at the base of a pond, but instead left behind by periodic localized floods. Such flooding still takes place today along the stream at Coats-Hines following heavy rainfall. The force of these regular events flushes tree branches, gravel, and debris along the channel and has undercut surrounding yards, prompting recent streambank mitigation efforts by the US Army Corps of Engineers.

By identifying and mapping the location and orientation of all of the bones and gravels in their excavation unit, the Texas A&M project concluded that the arrangement of those materials was also the result of moving water. Powerful, occasional flooding had forced bones, gravels, and debris through the stream drainage, along the way disarticulating and shifting animal skeletons. As bones and gravels tumbled against one another, the skeletal material became battered, abraded, and covered in scratches that are clearly visible on many larger bones from the site.

Twelve new radiocarbon dates from the 2012 project also help resolve questions about earlier dating efforts. All twelve dates, run on samples of charcoal created by natural wildfires, were recovered from soil levels that contained the animal bones. All returned dates older than 20,000 years BC. Out of the entire sample of twenty-one radiocarbon dates now run for the site, only two—one each from the 1994 and 2010 excavations—fall within the Paleoindian period. The overall radiocarbon data instead show that the bone bed at Coats-Hines formed between approximately 25,000 and 32,000 BC, millennia before the arrival of humans in the region.

As part of the 2012 effort, Tune also conducted new examinations of all the possible artifacts recovered from the site to date.[25] That study revealed some additional surprises. Natural processes, including being tumbled down a streambed and battered against other rocks, can cause flint nodules to fracture. Archaeologists therefore rely on specific physical characteristics created by the flintknapping process to determine the difference between natural stone breakage and human-made flint flakes. A reexamination of the site records showed that only twelve small flake fragments from 1994 had been recovered in situ, meaning "in their original place." Tune's assessment showed that none of the in situ objects exhibited the distinctive traits of flintknapping, and so none could be conclusively identified as human-made artifacts.

Tune's examinations of the original project field records revealed that all of the remaining flint fragments recovered in the 1990s came from bulk soil samples, and so were not directly associated with the animal bones. Reanalysis further showed that only two definite stone tools, a fragmentary knife or spear point and an angular stone scraper, were recovered during the 1994 excavations. Unfortunately, neither of those tools was excavated from a controlled context, so their association with the bone bed cannot be proven. Like the stone tools found in 2008, these may instead have originated from other, more recent archaeological deposits. A reassessment of the possible bone tools recovered in 1994 showed that, like the stone flakes, neither exhibited definitive evidence of human alteration. Finally, Tune showed that none of the stone fragments recovered at the site in 2010 or 2012 are conclusively artifacts rather than the results of natural stone fracturing. Contrary to early assertions, there have been no definitive human-made artifacts found in clear association with mastodon remains at Coats-Hines.

All this shows that the Coats-Hines site is not actually archaeological, but instead is a paleontological locale like those described by Troost. Although nearby sites show that Native Americans were present on the landscape surrounding Coats-Hines, there is no proof that they overlapped with, or hunted, ice age megafauna at that location. That said, there is still the question of the cut marks.

In the initial publication on the site, archaeologists reported possible cut marks on two bones: a vertebra and a humerus. By the following year those findings had been revised to list cut marks only on the vertebrae.[26] That bone was subsequently transferred on loan to the McClung Museum of Natural History and Culture in Knoxville, where it remains on display as part of their permanent exhibition "Archaeology and the Native Peoples of Tennessee."

Nearly three decades of archaeological science have passed since the initial identification of possible butchering marks at Coats-Hines, and in that time cut mark analysis has evolved to be a specialized field of archaeological study. Archaeologists now understand that other processes can create scratches, incisions, and marks on animal bone that in some cases are indistinguishable from those left by human activity. These notably include trampling by large animals like elephants, and natural movement or tumbling of bones against gravels. The vertebra from Coats-Hines has yet to be reevaluated by any archaeologist trained in cut-mark analysis, nor have the marks themselves been documented or described in the detail necessary for an independent evaluation of the original claims. It remains possible that future reexamination could conclude some of the marks on the Coats-Hines mastodon vertebra, or other bones from the site, were the result of human activity, and it is our hope that such a study will take place. In 2018, all of the animal remains from the site, except those on display at the McClung Museum, were transferred from the Division of Archaeology to the East Tennessee State University Center of Excellence in Paleontology for stabilization and curation at their Gray Fossil Site facility.

Fine Dining at the End of the Last Ice Age

After the First Americans arrived in the Western Hemisphere they would certainly have encountered, and on at least some occasions have hunted or scavenged, native megafauna. While we still tend to think of the First Americans as primarily big-game hunters, as our knowledge base of this time period grows it has become clear that there was no one-size-fits-all First American diet. Paleoindian period sites throughout the midcontinental United States have yielded culturally modified remains of many small animals, including turtles, fish, snakes, frogs or toads, gophers, birds, mice, lizards, voles, rabbits, shrews, deer mice, and aquatic snails.[27] That these animals were part of the Paleoindian diet is attested to by a variety of evidence, including direct association of their bones with hearths or trash deposits, and evidence of burning such as occurs during deliberate cooking rather than in natural fires. Many of these species live near water, and it's clear that the First Americans took advantage of the plants and animals that were commonly found in or near places where they could also find drinking water. Typically, these animals were small and easily captured—a pattern that might suggest the presence of families (instead of hunting parties) at these locations.

The late Pleistocene vegetation determined, to an extent, which herbivores lived in an area, which in turn determined the omnivores and carnivores that also lived there. Plant and animal communities were, and still are, interdependent, such that changes in one leads to changes in the other. Plant food evidence is very rare from Paleoindian period sites in the Eastern Woodlands of North America, and plant-processing tools are even rarer. One notable exception to this trend is the site of Dust Cave, located about ninety miles southeast of Nashville in Lauderdale County, Alabama.

Excavations at Dust Cave by archaeologists from the University of Alabama reveal that the site was periodically occupied over some 7,000 years, beginning ca. 10,700 BC during the late Paleoindian period.[28] The cave served as a regularly reused short-term encampment, offering ready access to fresh water, high-quality flint for making stone tools, wild game, and plant foods. Careful excavation techniques combined with excellent preservation in the cave have allowed archaeologists to recover evidence of a wide variety of plant resources in the form of seeds and nutshells. These debris from ancient meals eaten at Dust Cave paint a vivid picture of forager-hunter-gatherer life at the end of the last ice age.

Ancient Native American family groups, likely including multiple generations of extended kin, had intimate knowledge of life's basic necessities and where those resources could be found in the forests of the American Southeast. The most abundant plant foods eaten at Dust Cave, and by extrapolation also in Middle Tennessee, were those that were high in calories, or in protein and fats. The first category includes persimmons, grapes, and hackberries, while the second consists of hickory nuts, acorns, black walnuts, and hazelnuts. Excavations at Dust Cave uncovered several pit features, each of which contained more than a thousand acorn shells that had been cooked, dried, and then stored for later use. Preserved seed remains show leafy greens such as poke and chenopod were gathered in the early spring to offset a winter diet of stored nuts and meats.

Dust Cave is situated in the Mississippi Flyway, one of the well-known routes for birds traveling north on their spring migrations. Evidence for the hunting of migratory waterfowl, specifically Canada geese, ducks, and passenger pigeons, was found in the form of numerous bird bones in the cave deposits. The proximity to flowing freshwater meant ample opportunity to fish and capture other aquatic animals. However, in the Late Paleoindian deposits at Dust Cave, birds were among the most targeted animals.[29]

Mastodons very well may have been on the late ice age dinner menu in Tennessee and other parts of North America. However, there is a preponderance of physical evidence, in the form of animal bones, plant remains, and cooking features, that paint a picture of a more balanced First American diet. Although mastodons roamed around Middle Tennessee—which is pretty cool, to be honest—if we truly want to know about the meals prepared and eaten by the first Nashvillians, we need to keep digging.

CHAPTER 4

Modern Floods and Ancient Snailfishing on the Cumberland River

During the summer of 2009, children swimming along the water's edge of the Cumberland River, not ten miles from Lower Broadway, happened upon a human bone. That femur, the long bone from the upper leg, was lying in less than a foot of water near the base of a boat ramp. Metro police detectives arrived on the scene and quickly identified other human skeletal remains scattered along the nearby shoreline. The area was designated a possible crime scene, and police divers were dispatched into the river to look for further evidence. News crews arrived, and the story broke in the local media as authorities discovered and dragged out multiple cars that had been dumped in the Cumberland. After an exhaustive search, no further human remains were discovered, and there was no clear evidence of foul play.

As the news aired, phones began to ring at the Tennessee Division of Archaeology. Nashville's archaeological community was very familiar with that particular section of riverbank, which includes a large ancient Native American site. Although no professional archaeological investigations had ever taken place, shoreline erosion over the course of the twentieth century had exposed artifacts dating from the

FIGURE 4.1. Aaron inspects an Archaic shell midden exposed along the Cumberland River in Davidson County. Radiocarbon samples from this deposit show it was created between approximately 5000 and 4500 BC, as Native Americans deposited freshwater shellfish remains along the river's natural levee. Photograph by Jesse Tune.

Archaic, Woodland, and Mississippian periods. This single location along the Cumberland was the site of regular human occupation for over ten millennia, from around 9000 BC through AD 1300.

Large portions of the site visible along the riverbank consist of horizontal bands of freshwater shellfish remains, including both bivalves (mussels) and small aquatic gastropods (river snails). The shells in these deposits are incredibly densely packed, to the point that there is little soil present. In the 1970s, visible portions of the shell bands measured over twelve feet thick, but by 2009 steady erosion from weather and boat wakes had reduced the deposits to around just five feet in thickness (Figure 4.1).[1]

It is easy for casual observers to mistake shell deposits at sites along the Cumberland and Harpeth Rivers as being natural features rather than the result of human activity. For archaeologists, however, these locations stand out based both on the shells themselves, and other artifacts the sites contain. The river mussels and snail shells at these sites show evidence of human modification, including prying, piercing, and heating, and the mussels almost entirely consist of single valves that have been separated from their opposite halves. The dense shell layers also contain charred wood and nutshell, hearths and firepits lined with burned limestone, stone and bone tools, vertebrate animal remains, and sometimes, human burials. These types of archaeological deposits, traditionally known as "shell middens" or "shell mounds," appear throughout human history all across the world. Along the rivers of Tennessee and the American Southeast, shell middens mainly date to a phase archaeologists know as the Shell Mound Archaic, which stretches from about 7000 to 1000 BC.[2] On the Cumberland and Harpeth Rivers in Davidson, Cheatham, and Williamson Counties, shell midden sites date to between around 5900 and 1400 BC.

Following the 2009 discovery, Aaron visited the site with the Nashville medical examiner to determine if the human skeletal remains found by swimmers might be of archaeological origin. They found that recent, heavy rains had caused large sections of the riverbank to fall away, exposing nearly a dozen ancient Native American graves within and around the shell layer. Examination of burials still exposed in the riverbank showed those individuals had been buried in flexed (or fetal) positions with their knees pulled up toward their chests, an arrangement typical of the Archaic period.

The state archaeologist and the medical examiner determined that, since the graves had been exposed by natural processes, they should be left in place and not further disturbed by excavation. However, when Aaron visited the site several weeks later for a follow-up inspection, he found that no burials remained. Instead, pick and shovel scars pockmarked the riverbank where the graves had been looted, or illegally excavated, by individuals prospecting for artifacts. The human remains had been tossed down the riverbank, where some bones were still visible hanging in thick underbrush near the shoreline.

Less than a year after the discoveries at the boat ramp, a weekend of unprecedented weather pushed the Cumberland River in Middle Tennessee to a 1,000-year flood stage. The May 2010 floods had a profound impact on the lives of thousands of modern Nashvillians, as well as on the many archaeological sites in the area. At some locations, the force of floodwaters removed massive sections of riverbank, entirely erasing sites from existence or leaving behind only bare remnants. In other areas the flood exposed new site deposits that quickly attracted looters, who dug huge holes searching for artifacts, thereby further destroying the riverbank. While the damage caused by the 2010 flood and subsequent looting was significant, that catastrophic event also inspired and enabled some of the first professional archaeological studies of shell midden sites in Middle Tennessee. After nearly a decade of field and lab work, we now have entirely new and noteworthy understandings about the Native Americans who called Nashville home during the Archaic period.[3]

Understanding Archaic Period Nashville

Following the end of the last ice age, Earth entered the Holocene epoch, and global climates began a gradual warming trend that resulted in major changes to both plant and animal communities. Pollen and plant fossils collected from sediment cores at ponds in White and Franklin Counties show that by around 11,000 BC, Tennessee's environment had transitioned from predominantly mixed pine and spruce forests to a deciduous woodland dominated by oak, hickory, and ash.[4] The initial portion of this period also witnessed the final extinction of the megafauna discussed in previous chapters, and their replacement by the large animal species we are familiar with today, such as white-tailed deer, black bear, and gray wolf.

Humans had to adapt their technologies and diets to this new environmental reality. The cultural shifts that accompanied the early Holocene in the American Southeast culminated around 8000 BC with what archaeologists recognize as the beginning of the Archaic period. Foraging practices, including gathering, hunting, and fishing, developed during the late ice age and fine-tuned to Holocene environments successfully sustained Archaic period lifeways for the next 7,000 years.

Native Americans living in the Cumberland River valley of Middle Tennessee were particularly successful at negotiating the Pleistocene-Holocene transition. Populations in the region expanded dramatically, as shown by a rise in both the number and density of archaeological sites. A recent study of site data from the Cumberland River watershed between the Caney Fork and Harpeth Rivers found that the total number of archaeological sites in that region increased by more than 680 percent over the course of the Archaic period.[5]

As populations increased, community groups expanded into multi-family bands composed of several dozen individuals. Those groups were connected to other communities through emerging trade and social networks. Archaeological evidence suggests multiple bands would gather together periodically, perhaps annually, at large campsites along the Cumberland and Harpeth Rivers in order to exchange goods and bury their dead. For most of the rest of the year, those Archaic communities moved seasonally between campsites situated near reliable resource locations. Many sites were reoccupied regularly, in some cases over periods spanning thousands of years. However, there is not any archaeological evidence for the construction of permanent homes or structures at those locations.

Historically in Tennessee archaeology, academic and professional interest in Archaic period sites has lagged behind that shown toward more recent periods. This may be in part because of modern biases regarding certain artifact types and cultural behaviors. Western society traditionally places historical value on artworks, monuments, and social complexity. As a result, the forager-hunter-gatherer culture of the Archaic period in Middle Tennessee has been overshadowed by interest in the later Mississippian period. The finely made ceramic vessels, artwork, and earthen mounds found at many Mississippian sites all stoke the viewer's imagination. This is in contrast to Archaic period sites, which remain mostly hidden beneath the ground, and are therefore more difficult to envision.

During the late twentieth century archaeologists began to reconsider the Archaic period in eastern North America and to reexamine that era through a combination of new technologies and fresh ideas. These efforts have given us a better picture of Archaic period societies and led to the realization that their lifeways were far more complex than they had been previously credited for. Artifact studies have revealed Archaic period trade networks that exchanged both raw materials and specific artifact types between far-flung locations throughout the American Southeast. Construction of earthen mounds at sites such as Louisiana's Poverty Point, and the creation of shell mounds and rings along the Atlantic and Gulf coasts, suggests that large-scale site planning and social organization existed as early as 5,000 years ago.[6] Our own research in Middle Tennessee reveals further evidence of ritual complexity during the Archaic period, including the use of caves as burial sites, the creation and exchange of finely crafted artifacts, the symbolic importance of specific animal remains, and as mentioned in Chapter 1, the practice of tattooing.[7] Archaic period inhabitants of Nashville and the American Southeast were also engaged in the early stages of both plant domestication, and—as we will see—deliberate management of natural resources. All of these processes laid the essential groundwork for the agricultural societies of the subsequent Woodland and Mississippian periods.

Floods, Looting, and Archaeological Studies along the Cumberland

Thanks to efforts of local avocational archaeologists, we knew of several large, unstudied shell midden sites located near Nashville, and during the fall of 2009 we had visited those in the hopes of launching a new research project. It was the destruction we witnessed at those same sites after the 2010 flood that ultimately spurred us to study them more closely. During the weeks immediately following the flood, we revisited several of the shell sites to see how they had fared. To our dismay, we found not only extensive erosion caused by floodwaters, but also widespread destruction caused by illicit artifact digging.

Many Tennesseans collect artifacts, especially those which can be found on the surface of plowed agricultural fields or washed out along riverbanks. This practice is usually minimally destructive, and focuses on objects that have already been disturbed from their original archaeological context. Provided members of the public are not actively destroying an intact site by digging into it, have permission of the landowner, and are not disturbing graves or removing artifacts from municipal, state, or federal property, many archaeologists have minimal issues with the practice of artifact collecting. This is especially true when collectors share their knowledge with the archaeological community, thereby increasing our collective knowledge of the past. Collaborative efforts between Tennessee collectors and professional archaeologists have resulted in notable projects such as the Tennessee Fluted Point survey, which in turn informs the Paleoindian Database of the Americas discussed in Chapter 3.[8]

Unfortunately, not all those who collect ancient Native American artifacts are responsible or ethical. The term "looter" is reserved for individuals who illicitly dig holes into archaeological sites, typically in search of intact, finely made artifacts. Those objects are taken without any documentation of their original provenience, and with little or no care given to other archaeological data such as nutshell, animal bone, carbon fragments, or shellfish remains, all of which are discarded in their search. The artifacts most often sought by looters in Middle Tennessee include oversize spear points, carved bone and shell, and whole ceramic vessels, all of which are found mainly within ancient Native American graves. It is not uncommon for looters to hide, destroy, or discard Native American skeletal remains once they are done plundering a grave in order to obscure their actions and protect their so-called "honey holes" from notice by law enforcement, archaeologists, or other looters.

It would be nice if the same ethical standards and legal deterrents that keep people from digging up coffins in Nashville's City Cemetery to search for gold fillings and wedding rings would also apply to Native American graves. Regrettably, reality is more complicated. Once out of the ground, looted artifacts often become part of the regional antiquities black market, which is heavily connected to illegal activities including the manufacture and sale of methamphetamines. Over the past decade, Aaron's work at the Division of Archaeology has repeatedly involved cooperation with law enforcement agencies documenting archaeological artifacts and Native American skeletal remains seized during drug enforcement operations, and assessing damage to the sites from which those objects were illegally taken.

Within weeks of the 2010 flood we saw new looter excavations appear at riverbank sites throughout Davidson and Cheatham Counties. In some cases these pits extended more than fifteen feet along the riverbank and severely undercut the ground surface. With each subsequent rainfall, these holes caused more of the riverbank to collapse, further destroying private property and what remained of the archaeological sites.

The destruction of Middle Tennessee's archaeological heritage that we witnessed after the 2010 flood prompted us, along with our colleague Shannon Hodge, to apply for a Rapid Response grant from the National Science Foundation. These grants provide funding for scientific investigations in situations of extreme urgency, such as following

FIGURE 4.2. Archaeologists Shannon Hodge and Jesse Tune inspect an Archaic period site eroding from beneath a residential patio that overlooks the Cumberland River after the May 2010 flood. Artifacts recovered from this deposit show Native Americans lived at the site between about 7000 BC and AD 500. Image courtesy of the Tennessee Division of Archaeology.

natural disasters. With the support of that award we were able to conduct a survey of flood and looting damage at more than one hundred archaeological sites along the Cumberland River between Cheatham and Old Hickory dams (Figure 4.2).[9] From June through November 2010, our team of MTSU students and community volunteers logged hundreds of hours of field time and received invaluable assistance from organizations including Metro Nashville Parks, the Tennessee Wildlife Resources Agency, and the US Army Corps of Engineers.

Most of the sites we looked at following the 2010 flood had never been formally examined by professional archaeologists and were known only from limited artifact collections and word of mouth. The severe erosion and subsequent looting meant that details about the lives of the Native Americans who lived in these locations hundreds or thousands of years ago, details encapsulated in the bone, shell, and stone fragments, were forever lost. We were incredibly fortunate that, in addition to documenting the status of these sites, we were also able to salvage the only existing archaeological evidence of over a dozen locations in danger of imminent destruction.[10]

As a result of our survey project and months of archival research and artifact analysis, we determined that more than twenty archaeological sites between Cheatham Dam and Old Hickory Dam included thick deposits of freshwater shellfish remains. We were intrigued by these locations, which seemed almost unknown outside of the community of local avocational archaeologists. Entire scholarly books had been written on shell middens in the Ohio Valley, along Kentucky's Green River, and about the shell rings and mounds of Florida and Georgia. The sites along the Cumberland were virtually absent from the archaeological literature.

In 2012, Tanya directed a university-sponsored archaeological field school at one of the large Davidson County shell midden sites. That location had been inundated by the 2010 flood, exposing nearly 150 feet of shell deposits along the riverbank.[11] With the permission of the property owner, Tanya and her students undertook a seven-week field season to examine the site. As (bad) luck would have it, there was a heat wave that summer, during which temperatures reached over 100 degrees Fahrenheit for nearly ten days in a row. While enduring those record-breaking temperatures, twelve undergraduate anthropology majors from MTSU learned the basics of archaeological fieldwork.

Most modern archaeological investigations are limited in scope and focus on quality of data recovery and the complete analysis of those data, rather than the quantity of site exposed. Excavation destroys a site, and learning as much as possible about the past while doing minimal damage to the archaeological record has become a central tenet of archaeological science. Toward this end, Tanya's research design focused on the targeted capture of multiple types of data that could help answer both general and specific, long-term questions about Archaic shell midden sites in the region.

The first step in the project was to survey the river levee, using four-inch bucket augers to examine buried soils and thereby better understand the history of the landform. Ryan Robinson, a geoarchaeologist by training and now an archaeologist with the Tennessee Department of Transportation, led that effort to identify evidence of ancient flooding episodes, river course changes, and deeply buried archaeological deposits. All of the more than one hundred bucket auger tests went at least six feet deep, with a handful reaching about sixteen feet. At one point, Robinson decided to push the auger's capabilities and was able to reach just over thirty feet below ground surface. His efforts were rewarded with a four-inch diameter glimpse into the landscape as it formed and changed between the end of the last ice age and modern times, as well as bragging rights to having hand-excavated the deepest auger test recorded along the Cumberland River.

Tanya and her students used the results of Ryan's auger survey to place a series of excavation units where they could better collect data on different aspects of the site. Ultimately, Tanya and her team excavated a total site area of 344 square feet, with some test units reaching over six feet below ground surface. Although this is a considerable amount of dirt to move by hand, it represents only about 1 percent of the nearly acre-wide site. That project remains the only large-scale professional excavation of a shell midden site in the Nashville area. The results of the field school, combined with information from the post-flood survey and work by a contemporaneous archaeological project from the University of Tennessee, Knoxville, revealed substantial new information on Archaic period Nashville.

Archaic Snailfishing in Nashville

All but three of the shell midden sites in Middle Tennessee are located at river confluences, where the Cumberland or Harpeth are fed by

FIGURE 4.3. Pleurocerid (aquatic snail) remains from an Archaic period shell midden site along the Cumberland in Davidson County. Most of these shells belong to the armored rock-snail (*Lithasia armigera*), a species that makes up the majority of many Cumberland River shell middens. Photograph by Aaron Deter-Wolf.

one of their larger tributaries. As those waterways enter the Cumberland, they deposit their bedloads, the mix of sediment and gravels that accumulates along their path. Before the natural character of the river was changed in the twentieth century by channel dredging and dam construction, these confluences were marked by shallow, rocky shoals.

Shoals make up the natural habitats of many species of freshwater shellfish, including both river mussels and aquatic snails. Freshwater mussels of the biological family Unionidae are found worldwide but are especially diverse in the rivers of Tennessee and Kentucky. More than 150 unionid taxa are recorded in Tennessee, with eighty-five species identified in the Cumberland River basin. The many small, freshwater snails found in streams and rivers of Middle Tennessee are sometimes called "periwinkle" or "screw shells," and most often belong to the family Pleuroceridae (Figure 4.3). Pleurocerids are found only in Eastern North America and include more than 140 species.[12]

In our archaeological samples these snails range in length from about 0.17 to 1.6 inches. At Tanya's field site, one particular species of river snail stood out as being the most common, making up more than 80 percent of the total excavated gastropod remains. Today that species, the armored rocksnail (*Lithasia armigera*), only lives in two areas outside of the Ohio River Valley, and in Tennessee is found only in the Cumberland River.[13]

Freshwater shellfish presented a plentiful and easily accessible food source for ancient Native American inhabitants of Middle Tennessee. However, it was not until relatively recently that archaeologists recognized the possible long-term importance of these species to ancient diets. In the 1940s, archaeologists with the University of Tennessee and the Works Progress Administration conducted excavations at the Eva site, a large shell midden on the Tennessee River in Benton County. The investigators noted that while many remains of deer and other mammals were present above and below the shell midden, bones from those animals were virtually absent within the shell layers.[14] To explain these shifts, archaeologists suggested that severe droughts during the Archaic period had crashed the white-tailed deer population and caused game shortages. They postulated that in order to avoid starvation, ancient Native Americans turned to the shellfish beds made newly accessible by drought-reduced river levels. After the droughts passed, the river levels rose, deer populations rebounded, and people returned to their preferred food source. Over the next several decades, a similar consensus developed among many American archaeologists: that freshwater shellfish were a marginal food source, eaten only during times of environmental stress or when large game were not available. These attitudes were not entirely new, but rather based on several centuries of historical European and Euroamerican biases that considered Native American foraging, and shellfishing in particular, to be inherently "primitive" practices as compared to hunting game and farming.[15]

It is relatively easy for modern observers to embrace the idea of eating river mussels. A meal of freshwater snail is less familiar, and gastropod remains have been given especially short shrift in archaeological discussions. Well-researched shell midden sites from other areas, like those along Kentucky's Green River, are composed mainly of bivalve remains.[16] Prior to our 2010 survey it was assumed that the Cumberland River sites were also made up mostly of river mussels. Our research in Davidson and Cheatham Counties shows the opposite: that gastropods are overwhelmingly more abundant than bivalves in the Nashville-area shell middens.[17]

The sheer number of aquatic snails at some of the Cumberland River sites near Nashville is staggering. At Tanya's field school site, for example, we found that archaeological deposits of densely packed gastropod remains measured up to five feet thick in some areas. Combining the results of test excavations with data from the auger survey and a ground-penetrating radar study, we were able to estimate the site-wide number of gastropods at more than 360 million individuals. That does not include the portion of the site destroyed by the 2010 flood or by historical riverbank erosion. A cursory archaeological study of the same site done in 1988 found that, at that time, the shell midden extended over an additional acre.[18] By our estimates that portion of the site, now eroded into the Cumberland, probably included more than 370 million additional snail shells.

The millions of freshwater snails found in Cumberland River shell middens were not deposited overnight, or even over several decades. Radiocarbon samples collected by Tanya and her students show that, at their site, the shell deposit formed over a period of more than 2,000 years, between approximately 4900 and 2600 BC. Remarkably, there is no evidence of any interruption within the shell layers. If deposition of shellfish remains had stopped for an appreciable amount of time, plant growth and natural soil formation would have created a distinct layer, visible in the archaeological record as a band of soil stretching across the shell midden. No such soils are present at any of the shell midden sites we have examined along the Cumberland. This tells us that Archaic period snailfishing in the Nashville area was not a makeshift reaction to an environmental crisis. Instead, it was a sustainable lifeway continually practiced, in at least in one case, over at least eighty generations.

Ceramics and pottery were not part of the Archaic toolkit when the Cumberland River shell sites were occupied. The oldest pottery in the southeastern United States was made as early as 2500 BC in coastal communities of what is today Georgia, South Carolina, and northern Florida. That technology did not immediately gain widespread adoption outside those areas, and ceramics would not become standard in Middle Tennessee until after AD 200.[19] Instead most Archaic communities along the Cumberland relied on the same traditional technologies to carry, process, cook, store, and serve food that they had for millennia, including woven fiber or cane baskets, hide or skin bags, and wooden bowls or plates. These technologies decompose relatively quickly, and archaeological evidence for their use therefore comes mostly from sites with extraordinary preservation such as peat bogs and dry caves. Sadly, there are few intact sites like this in the American Southeast, fewer in Tennessee, and almost none in Nashville.

Because perishable Archaic technologies have not survived archaeologically, the specifics of shellfish cooking along the Cumberland River remain unclear. Preparations may have included simmering them by adding hot rocks to skin water bags, cooking by direct heat on stones above a hearth, or roasting in clay ovens or ash beds (Figure 4.4). Once cooked, snails could have been extracted from their shells using carved wooden toothpicks, a type of artifact that rarely survives in the archaeological record, while mussels would have been easily pried open with stone tools. Many of the snail remains from Tanya's field site exhibit single, small punctures in their outer whorls. These are not marks left by any of the snail's natural predators, and

FIGURE 4.4. View of an Archaic period feature containing burned stone, charcoal, and freshwater shells eroding along the Cumberland River near Nashville. The detail shows a few of the hundreds of freshwater snails it originally contained. This feature may be a location where shellfish were cooked. Photograph by Aaron Deter-Wolf.

we suspect they may instead have been made by people using stone or wooden tools to help remove the meat from the shells after cooking.

When considering ancient, pre-agricultural lifeways, it's tempting to reduce food to simply a search for calories. According to this logic, successful foraging brings in more calories than are expended in the search for food. In terms of energy, deer meat contains twice as many calories as freshwater shellfish, and therefore would seem to be a preferential food source.[20] But, as foodies know, meals are not just about calories. Freshwater snails provide higher amounts of calcium and iron than deer, while also being high in phosphorus, sodium, and potassium. People in the past lacked scientific laboratories in which to quantify the specific dietary benefits of their different foodstuffs, and instead created their foodways through generations of experimentation and familiarity with their local environment. By harvesting large quantities of snail remains, Archaic communities along the Cumberland were able to obtain essential nutrients—many of which are important for pregnant and breastfeeding women—not provided by the meat of deer or other terrestrial animals.

Food is necessary for life, and over the past 200,000 years humans have developed strategies to turn local plant and animal resources into dinner in nearly every ecological setting on Earth. Throughout time and across the world, these strategies have ranged from foraging, fishing, and hunting to the management and domestication of plants and animals, and ultimately to modern industrial agriculture. The traditional model of human history suggests that for nearly 99 percent of our past, people hunted wild animals and gathered wild plants on a seasonal basis, rather than actively managing food supplies or producing food through farming. The availability of these wild resources in turn influenced where and how people lived, population demographics, the invention of processing and storage technologies, and both social and gender dynamics.

Following the end of the ice age there was an increase in overall environmental and climate stability. Around the world, environments became more "zoned" along longitudinal lines, a concept reflected in the USDA agricultural zones. As the climate stabilized, humans gradually settled into certain locales on a full-time, year-round basis. Sustained interactions with local plants and animals resulted in what archaeologists call the Neolithic Revolution, the period during which many foraging societies shifted to being full-time farmers. That transition began as groups across the globe independently experimented with the management, and in some instances domestication, of plants and animals.

Not all societies followed the same path from foragers to farmers. Rather, people's interactions with their local environments resulted in specific skills and knowledge that, in various times and places, made agriculture possible. Decades of archaeological research have identified at least ten independent centers of plant and animal domestication, perhaps the best known of which was located in the Fertile Crescent region of the Middle East. In the Western Hemisphere, these centers include Central America, the Andes, and the midcontinental United States.

Beginning around 6000 BC during the Archaic period, Native American inhabitants of Middle Tennessee and eastern North America managed and eventually domesticated a group of plants known as the Eastern Agricultural Complex. The staples of that effort included squash, sunflower, and weedy greens like goosefoot, knotweed, and maygrass. Over recent decades archaeologists have come to recognize that Archaic period groups did not simply browse for these plants while traversing the landscape, but instead practiced environmental management strategies, including clearing and prescribed burning, to promote specific species on which they relied.[21]

Our research investigating Archaic shell midden sites along the Cumberland and its tributaries since the 2010 Nashville flood has led us to hypothesize that freshwater snail populations along the Cumberland River were also deliberately managed by Archaic period groups in order to ensure their long-term availability. As shown in Tanya's excavations, these efforts spanned millennia, coinciding with a period during which communities were becoming larger and less mobile, settling into specific areas, and beginning to experiment with plant domestication. If we are correct in our hypothesis, the multigenerational harvesting of river snails in the Cumberland River valley may be the earliest evidence for the practice of aquaculture in the Americas. Further archaeological research remains to be done, including additional geoarchaeological analysis and the sorting and detailed examinations of hundreds of thousands of additional snail shells.

Whether or not they were deliberately managing aquatic snail beds, Archaic period snailfishing along the Cumberland was an incredibly successful lifeway and sustained communities for over 3,000 years. The eventual end of this practice may be related to changes in the local environment caused by a massive flood. At Tanya's field site we discovered that, around 3200 BC, the Archaic shell midden at the upstream edge of the site was capped by a deposit of flood-borne, artifact-free soil measuring over nine inches thick. Shellfishing continued for some six centuries after that event, but during that time snail remains were deposited further away from the riverbank, and portions of the site that had been flooded were not reoccupied. By around 2600 BC, snailfishing ceased entirely, and the site was abandoned along with the other shell middens in Davidson and Cheatham Counties.[22] The practice briefly restarts around a millennia later at two Cumberland River sites near Nashville, but after that time communities appear to shift their shellfishing efforts east into Jackson and Smith Counties. Several of the Davidson County sites remained unoccupied for nearly 4,000 years, until the Mississippian period.

Archaeological research since the 2010 flood has revealed a new picture of Archaic period lifeways along the Cumberland River in Middle Tennessee. Unfortunately, even as we are learning this new information, the sites themselves have become critically endangered. Over the past decade we have witnessed the complete destruction of several Cumberland River shell midden sites, and we anticipate others will vanish in the near future as a result of extreme weather events, ongoing riverbank erosion, and looting. With these sites Nashvillians lose not just private and public property, but the final vestiges of a unique local culture history that lasted for over 3,000 years.

CHAPTER 5

Earthen Mounds
Meet Urban Sprawl

In 2017 controversy flared in Nashville surrounding a sweetheart deal to redevelop city-owned land along the margins of St. Cloud Hill, a promontory that overlooks the downtown core from the south. The land in question included the ruins of Greer Stadium, abandoned by the Nashville Sounds in 2014, and lay adjacent to Fort Negley Park, which protects and interprets a Civil War fort. The fort was constructed in late 1862 following the capture of Nashville by Union forces and built by a workforce of nearly three thousand conscripted laborers made up predominantly of formerly enslaved people. The fort was also the site of a United States Colored Troops encampment, and after the war the area around St. Cloud Hill became a thriving Black neighborhood.

Concerns of preservation groups and public outrage over the St. Cloud Hill project coalesced in part around historical research suggesting that graves of those who built the fort might still be located on city-owned property. The possible destruction or removal of Black graves at the site was viewed by many as continuing a legacy of oppression and suppressed history, and the story of how the New South engaged with historic cultural sites of its minority communities drew the attention of national media outlets.[1]

On the advice of Nashville's Metropolitan Historical Commission and the Division of Archaeology, Metro Parks and Recreation hired an archaeological consulting firm to examine the Greer Stadium property using remote sensing equipment. That study determined it was likely archaeological deposits were still present in the area, including beneath the stadium parking lots. The archaeologists conservatively and responsibly recommended that, given the history of the location, any intact archaeological deposits remaining on St. Cloud Hill might indeed include human remains or graves.[2] While no actual burials were ever identified on the site, the St. Cloud Hill project was ultimately abandoned in the face of community opposition. The events at Greer Stadium were seen as a win by preservationists and held up as encouraging evidence that modern Nashville was a city that could value and protect its multicultural past.

While the archaeological consideration, preservation, and protection afforded St. Cloud Hill is laudable, not all of Nashville's history is so lucky. Even as the Fort Negley controversy played out, a private development project in west Nashville went through the Chancery Court process to remove nearly 250 ancient Native American graves from a Mississippian period cemetery situated in the way of a planned dental office and plastic surgery center. The burial removal was conducted by a private archaeological firm, and the developer allowed the Tennessee Division of Archaeology to document and salvage only a small amount of archaeological data from the village site that surrounded those graves. There are no official metrics by which to compare, but this was likely the largest disinterment of Native American burials anywhere in the United States that year, and perhaps in more than a decade. Despite efforts by the Native American community, public concern and media interest in the cemetery removal were virtually nonexistent.

The west Nashville location is identified archaeologically as the Logan or Belle Meade site, and during the thirteenth and fourteenth

FIGURE 5.1. Mississippian ceramic effigy bottle from the Belle Meade/Logan site. The artifact measures 7.6 inches tall and is in a private collection. Photograph by Joseph Mohan, courtesy of Robert V. Sharp.

centuries AD was the site of a village that included dozens of single-family homes, several cemeteries, and at least one burial mound. The site has never received formal study but is well known locally as numerous graves have been exposed and dug into by the interested public during construction of the surrounding neighborhood and businesses throughout the mid-twentieth century. A number of marine shell, copper, and ceramic artifacts taken from the site over the years now reside in private collections (Figure 5.1).

The Logan site is not unique, either in terms of scale or in its destruction at the hands of modern development. Today's Davidson County is built atop more than 130 Mississippian period communities that date to between about AD 1000 and 1475. The largest of these were a half dozen large towns, built surrounding groups of earthen mounds that served as burial locations or platforms for elevated structures. More than sixty smaller Mississippian towns and villages were also situated throughout Nashville, some of which were protected behind log palisade walls and might include one or two mounds. Regardless of their size or the number of mounds they contained, these sites all included homes, workshops, religious structures, public spaces, and cemeteries.

A visitor arriving in downtown Nashville via the Cumberland River in the thirteenth century AD would have gravitated not to the lights of lower Broadway, but to the East Nashville Mounds. That site was focused on a chain of four earthen mounds that overlooked the east bank of the Cumberland, near the location of Cowan and Jefferson Streets. The area immediately surrounding the mounds was dense with Mississippian period occupation, and in 1876, Nashville health officer and antiquarian archaeologist Joseph Jones noted that erosion along the Cumberland riverbank in the area "constantly exposes stone graves, skeletons, and relics of various kinds."[3]

From the mounds, the village extended almost a mile north through McFerrin Park to Cleveland Street.[4] Directly across the river at Sulphur Dell sat another mound, surrounded by residences and cemeteries that spread through today's Germantown neighborhood and Bicentennial Capitol Mall State Park. Salt processing areas, rediscovered in 2014 during the construction of the new Nashville Sounds baseball stadium, lay along the banks of Lick Branch, and to the south, a Mississippian period cemetery was located on the crest of Capitol Hill.

Other Mississippian period towns and villages were situated at approximately two to three mile intervals throughout Davidson County, including at Moss Rose Drive, on Richland Creek near Aquinas College, at Travellers Rest, and on Bells Bend, Cockrill Bend, and Neeleys Bend. Still others were located along historic trading paths that today correspond to Brick Church Pike, Gallatin Pike, Whites Creek Pike, and the Natchez Trace. The northern end of the Natchez Trace at Cockrill Spring was the site of a large Mississippian town destroyed by historical development of Centennial Park and the surrounding West End neighborhood.

The landscape in between these larger sites was filled with small family farmsteads such as those that filled Shelby Bottoms. This pattern continues beyond Davidson County, stretching into Cheatham, Sumner, and Williamson Counties and particularly along the Harpeth River watershed. As a whole, Middle Tennessee was home to more than 330 known Mississippian communities, around 36 of which included earthen mounds (Figure 5.2). These were not independent, isolated sites, but situated within what we today recognize as an interconnected urban landscape.

Archaeologists don't yet have a firm estimate as to exactly how many people lived in Mississippian-era Nashville, but by all indications the numbers were impressive. Along Brown's Creek near Lipscomb University, the site known as Noel Cemetery once included more than three thousand Mississippian period graves. In 1823, when describing Mississippian period cemeteries in what is today the Germantown

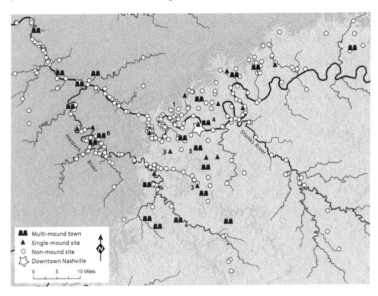

FIGURE 5.2. Map of Mississippian sites in the Nashville area, showing major sites mentioned in the text: (1) Averbuch, (2) Brentwood Library, (3) Logan, (4) East Nashville Mounds, (5) Noel Cemetery, and (6) Mound Bottom State Archaeological Area.

neighborhood, Judge John Haywood estimated that "a population once resided here, which more than twenty times exceeded that of the present day."[5] Haywood's estimate involves some very nonscientific, back-of-the-envelope calculations, but would put the total Mississippian period population of Nashville at around 400,000, a number not achieved again until the 1960s.[6]

"The Moundbuilders"

So who were the people that built these mounds and villages and created Nashville's first urban core? They were, of course, Native Americans. Some were probably the descendants of people who had lived in Middle Tennessee since the late Pleistocene and who built the Archaic period shell mounds along the Cumberland River. Others, as we'll see, may have come to the Cumberland River valley from different areas. Archaeologists broadly identify ancient Native American cultures in Tennessee beginning about AD 1000 as belonging to the Mississippian period, based on a suite of artifacts and lifeways that coalesce over a vast area of the eastern United States. These traits include construction of large-scale permanent towns and villages; reliance on full-time farming of maize, beans, squash, and other crops; formation of a highly organized, ranked society; manufacture of ceramics using local clay tempered with crushed freshwater shells; and the widespread construction of earthen mounds.

Popular discussions of Mississippian culture in Tennessee and beyond sometimes reference Mississippian period people as the Moundbuilders, a term whose genesis lies in historical misconceptions of American prehistory. During the nineteenth century, the origins of the ancient earthen mounds found throughout eastern North America were considered a great mystery. The earthworks were known to predate the contemporaneous Native American tribes, who did not have specific, first-hand knowledge of their construction. Moreover, many Euromerican scholars, blinded by the biases of their day, regarded living Native Americans and their ancestors as being too "primitive" to have ever built such monuments or created the artifacts they contained. Instead North America's earthen mounds were variously attributed to outside groups including the ancient Welsh, Toltecs, Aztecs, Vikings, the Lost Tribes of Israel, or a vanished race of either giants or "pygmies," depending on the source.

The Moundbuilder myth, as it is known today by archaeologists, was created during the nineteenth century in order to explain the unknown. However, it also marginalized Native Americans, reinforcing racist stereotypes regarding their cultural complexity and casting them as interlopers and invaders. According to the logic underpinning the Moundbuilder myth, if Native Americans had not constructed the mounds, then they must have either killed or forced out those who did. This theory was not just idle speculation but instead was used to justify historical seizures of Native lands. In his second annual message to Congress on December 6, 1830, President Andrew Jackson invoked the Moundbuilder myth while praising the legislature for passing the Indian Removal Act: "In the monuments and fortresses of an unknown people, spread over the extensive regions of the west," he wrote, "we behold the memorials of a once powerful race, which was exterminated, or has disappeared, to make room for the existing savage tribes."[7]

The Indian Removal Act codified the Jackson administration's desired policy of removing Native Americans from their traditional homelands to territories west of the Mississippi River, on the journey that came to be known as the Trail of Tears. In 1838, thousands of Cherokee passed through downtown Nashville along one Trail of Tears route. That group came through Public Square and crossed over the Cumberland on a toll bridge. The footings of that bridge still exist and were rediscovered in 2012 alongside the Woodland Street Bridge by the Native History Association.[8] After crossing the river, the Cherokee turned north on the old Whites Creek Road, which ran along the riverbank directly through the East Nashville Mounds site.[9] It's not clear from the historical record if any aboveground remnant of the site remained visible at the time.

Although the Moundbuilder myth is steeped in pseudoscience, historical misunderstandings, and racism, it continues to be perpetuated in modern, popular works of pseudoarchaeology. Some of these rely on fantastic, unsupported claims to suggest that America's ancient mounds were built by groups including the Maya, Egyptians, or citizens of Atlantis. Others claim that the original inhabitants of North America were a light-skinned (tacitly European) race, who were the progenitors of ancient civilizations and advanced technology all across the world before the impact of one or more comets cleared the way for later Native Americans. To be clear: there is absolutely no legitimate archaeological, linguistic, or biological evidence that the ancient occupants of North America or the Cumberland River valley were anyone other than ancestral Native Americans, nor is there any valid suggestion that they needed special assistance from far-flung civilizations (or extraterrestrials) to create their monuments, artifacts, and societies.

Mississippian Archaeology in Greater Nashville

During the nineteenth century, antiquarian scholars and early archaeologists recognized that archaeological materials from the Nashville area were different from discoveries made at ancient mound sites elsewhere in North America. One of the main traits they noted in this regard was the density of "stone box graves" in Middle Tennessee. Stone box graves are essentially coffins fashioned from slabs of undressed tabular limestone. The floors of those Mississippian period graves are sometimes lined with stone, pottery, or mussel shells, and individuals buried within them usually lie in an extended position on their backs. In any given cemetery or burial mound, stone box graves might be placed separately from one another, be so close as to share a wall, or even cut across earlier graves. In some instances stone boxes were reopened and reused, with new burials placed atop the earlier occupant(s), or older remains moved to the side.

The aesthetic quality of ceramic, shell, and stone artifacts sometimes included in these graves led to their being historically targeted by both private collectors and representatives of nationally known institutions, including the Peabody Museum at Harvard and the Bureau of American Ethnology. In addition to these deliberate disturbances, thousands of stone box graves were exposed or destroyed by agriculture and development throughout the nineteenth and early twentieth century. The frequency of these encounters in the Nashville area led some antiquarian scholars to identify the ancient inhabitants of the region as the "Stone Grave Peoples" or the "Stone Grave race of Middle Tennessee."[10]

Bob Ferguson was the first modern archaeologist to attempt to define the unique Mississippian tradition from the Nashville area. In a 1972 publication describing salvage excavations at two village sites destroyed by subdivision construction, Ferguson identified the Mississippian groups that lived in the Cumberland River valley, from the confluence with the Caney Fork downstream to the Ohio River, as belonging to "the Middle Cumberland Culture."[11] Within that area he noted the presence of large numbers of stone box graves, mound sites, and specific styles of shell-tempered ceramic vessels.

Most of the archaeological work at Mississippian sites in Middle Tennessee over the last forty years has been instigated by modern development. Excavations at some sites during the 1990s, including at Fewkes Mounds in Brentwood and at the East Nashville Mounds, was done according to federal permitting requirements described in Chapter 1. Efforts at other sites, including Moss Wright Park, Travellers Rest, Old Town, Noel Cemetery, Sulphur Dell, and Logan, were intended to identify and remove Mississippian period graves under Tennessee's Cemetery Statutes. Those burial removal projects were typically performed by private archaeological firms, and depending on the situation and the consultant, often included little attempt to recover non-burial data, or even to record sites with the Division of Archaeology. The destruction of thousands of undocumented Mississippian period artifacts and features during cemetery removal projects since the 1980s represents an incalculable loss to Nashville's history.

Because most modern excavations at Mississippian period sites in Nashville have been related to development efforts, their scope has been limited to specific construction footprints. As a result, archaeologists have had very small windows into much larger sites. For example, excavations for the Jefferson Street Bridge project in the 1990s studied only the bridge footings and approach. Beneath several feet of historical fill in those locations, archaeologists identified dozens of Mississippian pit features, postholes, house footprints, and stone box graves associated with the East Nashville Mounds site. As already described, historical accounts give us some idea as to the original extent of that town, which may have covered several hundred acres along the east bank of the Cumberland. No archaeological studies were performed in 2016 during construction of the Top Golf facility, located just a few hundred feet north of the bridge. While the East Nashville Mounds site certainly extended into that area, we will never know what may have been encountered and lost during construction. As of spring 2021, no archaeological investigations are planned for either the adjacent River North or East Bank development areas, both of which fall within the likely extent of the Mississippian town.

What we understand today about the Mississippian period in Nashville is in large part the result of decades of research and collaboration by MTSU anthropology professor Kevin Smith and Tennessee state archaeologist (now retired) Mike Moore. Moore grew up in Nashville, and after attending graduate school in Oklahoma, returned to Middle Tennessee for a job at the Division of Archaeology. Smith, also from Tennessee, attended graduate school at Vanderbilt, where his PhD dissertation mined the antiquarian literature to craft the first major synthesis of Mississippian period settlement in what he called the Middle Cumberland Region.[12]

In the 1990s both Smith and Moore worked under then state archaeologist Nick Fielder at the Division of Archaeology, where they began their long-term partnership investigating Mississippian period Nashville. Over the next three decades Smith tracked down artifact collections and unpublished historical accounts of sites in Middle Tennessee, and was part of working groups devoted to deciphering Mississippian art and iconography. For over a decade he led MTSU's archaeological field school at Castalian Springs Mounds State Archaeological Area in Sumner County. That project is one of the few modern investigations of a Mississippian period site in Middle Tennessee not initiated in response to, or limited in scope by, development concerns.

FIGURE 5.3. Mississippian strap handle ceramic bowl, with a label reading "Found on Dr. W. H. Jarmans Farm near Brentwood Tenn." This artifact from the collection of Vanderbilt University is likely one of those excavated by Jarman and donated to the school before his death. Photograph by Kevin E. Smith.

Moore directed numerous salvage and testing projects for the Division of Archaeology during the 1990s, including at Mississippian farmstead and village sites that were ultimately destroyed by suburban development. One of those projects was at the Brentwood Library, located along the Little Harpeth River in Williamson County.[13] The Brentwood Library site is notable in that it presents an excellent example of a fortified Mississippian village, as well as in how its story encapsulates the progression of archaeological interest in the region.

The property that is today the James P. Holt Brentwood Library was purchased by Dr. William H. Jarman in February 1880. Jarman, like many wealthy, educated men of his era, had a personal interest in antiquities. After acquiring the farm, he discovered that it contained artifacts and stone box graves, and he collected an assortment of ceramic, bone, and stone artifacts from the property (Figure 5.3).[14] In enthusiasm for his discoveries, Jarman wrote to Frederic Ward Putnam, the curator of the Peabody Museum at Harvard University.[15] Putnam had visited Nashville three years earlier, when for several months he conducted excavations of mounds and graves at large Mississippian sites including Travellers Rest, Bowling Farm (today on the grounds of Aquinas College), Brick Church Pike Mounds, and Sellars Farm State Archaeological Area.

In 1882, Putnam traveled to Williamson County where, with the assistance of his foreman George Woods, Tennessee's first professional Black archaeologist, he excavated nearly ninety stone box graves in the immediate area of the Jarman home.[16] Among the artifacts recovered from those burials for the collections of the Peabody Museum were carved marine shells, ceramic vessels, and according to Putnam, "immense numbers of stone implements or weapons."[17] Many of the ceramics were effigy forms, including bowls and jars made to resemble gourds, frogs, and fish, along with bottles shaped like owls and humans, or at least human-like-characters. Although Putnam described his excavations in several short publications, the exact location of what he called the Jarman Farm or Brentwood site was subsequently forgotten.

In July 1997, construction had just begun at the City of Brentwood's new public library on Concord Road. Substantial grading had taken place across the property, and a rock pad laid for the library foundation, when a construction worker noticed a stone box grave. The head librarian notified the Division of Archaeology, and on inspecting the site, Moore and his colleagues identified numerous other stone box graves and archaeological features throughout the construction site. Historical deed research subsequently identified the property as having been owned by Dr. Jarman, whose house once stood a short distance south of the planned library building.

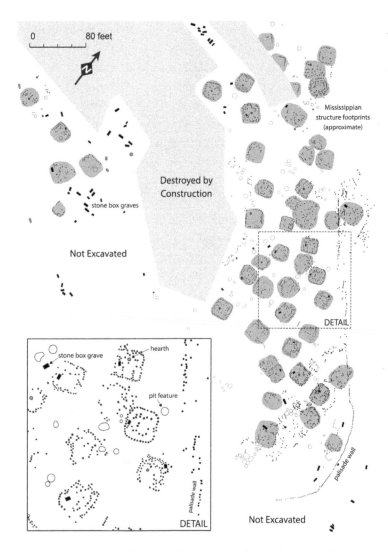

FIGURE 5.4. Excerpt of the Brentwood Library site map, showing the portion of the Mississippian period village encountered during library construction. Image courtesy of the Tennessee Division of Archaeology.

The city was granted a Chancery Court order allowing for removal of graves within the project area, and hired a private archaeological consultant to do that work. As described in Chapter 1, such projects are not obligated to recover or address any archaeological aspects of a site other than human burials. In the case of the library site, the City of Brentwood granted permission to the Division of Archaeology to record and evaluate exposed non-burial features, so long as the removal project was ongoing.

Moore directed archaeologists from the Division of Archaeology and volunteers who worked for four months to identify, document, and, wherever possible, excavate portions of more than five thousand archaeological features. Those included the footprints of sixty-seven houses, more than 2,500 pit features, and a portion of a defensive palisade wall (Figure 5.4). During that same period the archaeological consultant identified more than eighty graves, over two-thirds of which were removed to make way for construction. In total, more than ten thousand artifacts from the site were recovered, catalogued, identified, and analyzed.

Site maps can be difficult to interpret for non-archaeologists because of the amount of detailed information they contain. The map of the Brentwood library site shows the clustering of densely packed, single-family homes just inside, and sometimes overlapping, the northeast corner of the site's defensive palisade wall. The house footprints are roughly square, and average around 430 square feet. They are visible on the map as arrangements of dozens of small circular features, each marking where a wooden post was once set upright in the ground. Exterior posts were intertwined with river cane and covered in clay to create wattle and daub walls. Posts in the building's interior held up roofs consisting of cane or woven matting.

Most homes included a single interior hearth, usually centered roughly within the structure to vent smoke out the roof peak. Because of this arrangement, house fires were not an unusual occurrence, and many of the structures at Brentwood Library and other Mississippian period sites include multiple lines of wall posts showing where burned homes were repaired or rebuilt entirely over time. Some houses included single stone box graves beneath their floors that held the remains of children. Adults were typically buried in cemetery areas within the village, identifiable on the map as clusters of stone box graves.

The amount of data recovered from the Brentwood Library project is impressive, but the investigated portion of the site represents probably less than a third of the total village. Only one corner of the palisade was discovered during the excavations, and we know the site once extended at least four hundred feet south to the area where Jarman's house stood. What was learned is therefore just a small glimpse into the Native American community that lived at this village from about AD 1250 to 1450. It would take years to properly excavate and document a complete site of this size and complexity to the standards of modern scientific archaeology. While it is incredibly fortunate that the Division of Archaeology was able to gather this information on the Brentwood Library site, the sum of the acquired knowledge is only a drop in the bucket compared to the complete site remains.

From their research at sites like Brentwood Library and in the collections of the Peabody Museum, Smith and Moore have demonstrated that the Middle Cumberland Mississippian is indeed a unique regional culture within the greater Mississippian sphere. Using distributions of ceramic styles, they have refined the boundaries of the culture to include the Cumberland River watershed from approximately Dixon Springs in Smith County downstream to Big McAdoo Creek in Montgomery County.[18] The central portion of this area, and the major focus of Mississippian period occupation, are today's Davidson and Williamson Counties. In 2009, Moore and Smith compiled the archaeological data to propose a new chronology for the

Middle Cumberland Mississippian.[19] That framework provides us with a better understanding as to the formation, spread, and decline of Nashville's final pre-European contact culture.

The Middle Cumberland Mississippian

Around AD 1000, the population gradually began to increase along the Cumberland and Harpeth Rivers, and construction began at some of the first Mississippian multi-mound sites in the region, including Mound Bottom State Archaeological Area in Cheatham County. Mound Bottom would ultimately feature twelve mounds surrounding a seven-acre plaza, all situated within a tight meander bend of the Harpeth River. Less than a mile away, the contemporaneous Pack site spread over several hundred acres and included around twenty mounds and a series of small plazas. No archaeological work has been done at Pack since 1937, while in 2016, Aaron directed the first excavations at Mound Bottom in over forty years.[20] Based on the evidence to date, archaeologists believe that Mound Bottom and Pack likely represent separate portions of a single, larger site.[21]

When construction began at Mound Bottom and Pack in the late tenth century AD, there was virtually no local precedent for their eventual size. No similar multi-mound centers had existed in the Nashville area for more than five hundred years, since the Woodland period Glass Mounds site near Franklin. The scale of construction and level of planning at Mound Bottom and Pack suggests both the presence of a directed labor force and a level of centralized political or social organization not evident in the area for several centuries prior. Artifacts recovered from Mound Bottom and Pack have led Smith, Moore, and others to propose that those sites may have been built by, or at least at the behest of, people who moved to Middle Tennessee from the American Bottom region of the Mississippi River Valley, and perhaps from the site of Cahokia Mounds.[22]

Cahokia Mounds is a National Historic Landmark and UNESCO World Heritage Site near modern day Saint Louis, Missouri, and has been called the "first native city in North America."[23] While archaeologists quibble about the precise definition of "city," Cahokia is unrivaled in its status as the largest ancient Native American site in the eastern United States. The site's two-hundred-acre core is located east of the Mississippi River in Collinsville, Illinois, and focused on Monks Mound, which today stands at one hundred feet tall and is the largest pre-Columbian structure north of the Rio Grande. This central area of the site is surrounded by dozens of satellite towns and villages, for a total metropolitan area covering more than three thousand square miles on both sides of the Mississippi. At its peak in the thirteenth century AD, Cahokia was larger in both size and population than contemporary London, with a sphere of influence that stretched throughout the midcontinental and southeastern United States, extending as far west as Oklahoma. It appears that Cahokia did not exercise direct political control over these other areas, but instead inspired and influenced regional cultural development.[24]

Cahokian influence is evident throughout Middle Tennessee, as seen in the presence of specific artistic styles, iconographic designs found on ceramic and marine shell artifacts, and "symbolic weaponry"—oversized, finely made stone weapons used as elite regalia rather than actual tools of war. These artifacts have been recovered from a number of early Mississippian mound centers along the Cumberland and Harpeth Rivers, and archaeologists believe they were made and distributed as a means of establishing political ties between sites.

Populations in the Middle Cumberland region expanded substantially during the two centuries following initial construction at Mound Bottom and Pack. Between about AD 1100 and 1200, both those sites grew in size and extended their influence eastward across the Nashville area. Several other large towns and villages were also founded during this period, including along Richland Creek in west

Nashville, at Sellars Farm State Archaeological Area near Lebanon, and at Fewkes Mounds in Brentwood.

New settlements continued to proliferate throughout the Nashville area during the thirteenth century. Moore and Smith's analysis suggests that more large villages were founded during this period, including at Noel Cemetery and throughout the Little Harpeth watershed. Several of those sites include one or more earthen mounds and large cemetery areas, suggesting they enjoyed some degree of political independence from Mound Bottom and Pack.

Even as populations expanded, people in the Middle Cumberland region were experiencing both environmental and social stress. In their ongoing research, Tennessee scholars including Smith, David Dye (University of Memphis), and Lynne Sullivan (University of Tennessee, Knoxville) are working to connect Mississippian period cultural change in the thirteenth and fourteenth centuries AD with environmental shifts taking place in Middle Tennessee and throughout the American Southeast.[25] Those efforts rely in part on regional tree-ring chronologies reconstructed in the North American Drought Atlas.[26]

As trees grow, their annual rings record local climate patterns. During warm, wet years faster tree growth results in wider rings. During cold and dry periods, and particularly during droughts, tree growth is slow and results in more closely spaced rings. One metric that uses tree ring data to examine past climates is the Palmer Drought Severity Index (PDSI).[27] That index employs a sliding scale to estimate how much soil moisture was available in a region during a given period. Archaeologists working with these data have further classified PDSI values to identify when a region likely experienced normal, minimal, or failed harvests.[28] According to those models, minimal harvests likely resulted in enough food to support the local population on an annual basis, but yielded little or no surplus. A year of crop failure followed by a year of minimal harvest, or two consecutive years of failed harvests, would have resulted in depletion

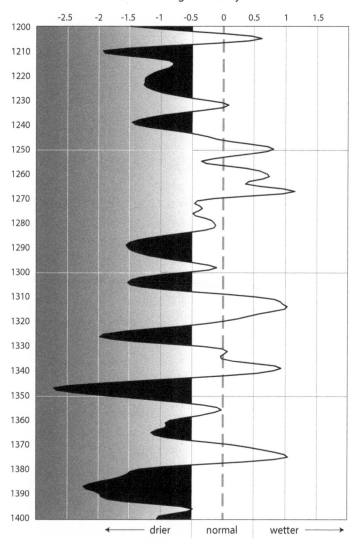

FIGURE 5.5. Drought cycles for Middle Tennessee during the thirteenth and fourteenth centuries AD, based on the Palmer Drought Severity Index. The values are smoothed over ten-year intervals to better illustrate decade-long trends, with black-filled peaks indicating periods of drought.

of reserves and led to food shortfalls. The PDSI is not a definitive reading of past climate cycles, but when compared to archaeological information, the climate data reveals some interesting patterns for Middle Tennessee. In the Nashville area, PDSI levels recorded in the North American Drought Atlas suggest the region experienced erratic rainfall cycles throughout the thirteenth and fourteenth centuries AD (Figure 5.5). Drought conditions persisted for more than half of the thirteenth century, culminating in seventeen minimal and five failed harvests between AD 1284 and 1309.

Archaeological evidence from the Nashville area suggests that during this same time the Middle Cumberland region also witnessed an increase in interpersonal violence. Mississippian period skeletal remains show more instances of scalping and cranial blunt force trauma during the late thirteenth and early fourteenth centuries as compared to among earlier populations.[29] There is not yet any archaeological evidence of battles, massacres, or mass graves, perhaps indicating that the uptick in interpersonal violence reflects cultural or societal stress rather than organized raiding and warfare.

Early in the fourteenth century a substantial palisade wall was built at the Pack site, separating it from the nearby center at Mound Bottom. Shortly thereafter, probably by around AD 1350, both Mound Bottom and Pack were mostly vacated. Both sites continued to be used as burial locations but were no longer home to full-time residents. Instead, Mississippian populations in Middle Tennessee coalesced in large, fortified towns like Brentwood Library and Averbuch. The log palisades at those sites sometimes include regularly spaced bastions that would have allowed defenders to fire along the walls. Archaeologists have not yet discovered clear evidence for any direct attacks on fortified settlements in the Middle Cumberland, but the residents of the region were clearly anticipating trouble. Some fortified villages of this time included single mounds, or in the case of Fewkes Mounds in Brentwood, occupied the same location as earlier multi-mound centers. However, construction of new earthen mounds in Middle Tennessee ended during the early fourteenth century.

Archaeologists currently interpret these shifts in where and how Mississippian communities lived as being symptomatic of political destabilization, as large chiefdom centers were replaced by smaller, more autonomous villages. The collapse of centralized authority seems to have occurred relatively rapidly at first glance, but was probably related to decades of ongoing drought and food insecurity. Between AD 1300 and 1350 the Middle Cumberland region suffered twenty-one minimal and ten failed harvests, five of which occurred back-to-back beginning in 1346 (see Figure 5.5). Over the second half of the fourteenth century, nearly two-thirds of harvests produced no surplus. In AD 1379, back-to-back failed harvests depleted any accumulated stores and ushered in another sixteen years of drought. By the end of the fourteenth century, all crop surpluses in the Middle Cumberland had long since vanished.

The cumulative impacts of decades-long environmental and cultural stress are directly reflected in the health of those buried in fourteenth-century Middle Cumberland cemeteries. In addition to rising interpersonal violence, people began to suffer from increased rates of anemia, enamel hypoplasia, dental abscesses, and tooth loss, as well as diseases such as tuberculosis.[30] Overall mortality rates also increased throughout the region during the fourteenth century. At the Averbuch site, life expectancy was only around sixteen years at birth, extending to around twenty-two years for those who survived childhood.[31] At Brentwood Library, the overall infant mortality rate is calculated to have been nearly 50 percent.[32]

It was during this same period that the burial of infants within homes became standard practice throughout the Nashville area (see Figure 1.4). Almost a quarter of the houses examined at Brentwood Library included one or more infant burials. In his analysis of Middle Cumberland ceramic vessels, Smith has noted that many infant graves from the second half of the fourteenth century include effigy vessels depicting aquatic creatures such as fish, frogs, river mussels, and ducks. It is compelling to think that the inclusion of these objects in children's graves represents a religious or spiritual effort by parents and survivors to break the ongoing droughts.

The population of the Nashville area began to decline toward the end of the fourteenth century in the face of an ongoing environmental crisis. The region went on to suffer fifty-one years of drought over the course of the 1400s, with a decade-long period beginning in AD 1449 that included seven failed harvests. There is little archaeological evidence that the Nashville area was permanently occupied after AD 1475, although recent statistical analysis of radiocarbon data from the region suggests occupations at some sites may have persisted until the early 1500s.[33] We do not yet understand the details as to where populations relocated after this time, although artifact similarities suggest both southeast Tennessee and southern Missouri as possible candidates.[34]

The fifteenth-century collapse of Mississippian political structures is not restricted to the Nashville area. Tree ring data, along with historic temperature and precipitation evidence preserved in lake sediments, suggest that similar environmental conditions during the mid- to late fourteenth century led to multi-year crop failures and food insecurity throughout much of America's Eastern Woodlands.[35] Around this time the Gulf Stream that previously had drawn moisture-rich air northward weakened, allowing cold, dry air from the Arctic to spread across the northern latitudes. This lowered average temperatures by around 2 degrees Fahrenheit and ushered in a period known as the Little Ice Age.[36] During this period large portions of the Tennessee, Ohio, and Mississippi river watersheds also underwent political turmoil, culminating in a widespread pattern of regional abandonment that archaeologists refer to as the Vacant Quarter.[37] To the north at Cahokia, population declined gradually over the thirteenth century, and the site appears to be entirely vacated by around AD 1400.

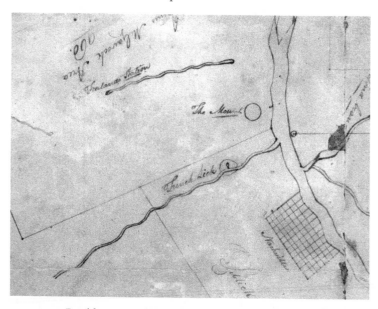

FIGURE 5.6. Detail from a map of plantations along the Cumberland River, drawn by David McGavock in 1786. The Mississippian mound that served as the base for the French stockade is shown west of the Cumberland River on McGavock's nine-hundred-acre plot and labeled "The Mount." From the Tennessee State Library and Archives, no. 42829_01, "Sketch of plantations along Cumberland River (Nashville and surrounding land, 1786)."

While the climate data is compelling, droughts alone cannot explain the ultimate fracturing of Mississippian period societies. By the beginning of the fifteenth century Native Americans and their ancestors had lived along the Cumberland River and its tributaries in Middle Tennessee for over thirteen thousand years. During that vast expanse of time they domesticated plants and animals, organized and reorganized their society, invented new technologies, and actively managed their local environment. The end of the Mississippian period was not a sudden, dramatic rupture, but a complicated and gradual affair that took place over more than two centuries. Ultimately, decades of food insecurity probably exacerbated ongoing social and political stress, combining to push already-troubled societies over the edge.

When Martin Chartier and other early French traders arrived at Sulphur Dell in the seventeenth century AD, they entered a region that was empty of permanent Native American settlement. The area was not void of Native presence, however, and the early Europeans interacted with tribes including the Shawnee, Cherokee, Chickasaw, and Muscogee. None of these groups seem to have resettled Mississippian sites in the Nashville area, at least so far as has been documented archaeologically to date, with one exception. In Germantown, a Mississippian period mound formerly stood just to the north of the modern Jefferson Street Bridge (Figure 5.6). When the first Europeans arrived at French Lick they found the mound surrounded by a stockade, which they attributed to the Shawnee. The defensibility and proximity of that location to the salt spring was attractive to the Europeans, and the mound was subsequently refortified for use as a trading post by historical figures including Chartier, Jean du Charleville, and Timothy Demonbreun. The first inkling of modern Nashville was built, quite literally, atop the ancient Native American past.

The Past and Present Meet in Nashville

By the late 1990s the archaeological community believed that few large Mississippian town or village sites remained undisturbed in Middle Tennessee. The legacy of Nashville's ancient Native American history that had begun to wane in the thirteenth century had apparently resolved some seven hundred years later at the hands of modern development. At that time it seemed that all of the large Mississippian period sites described by antiquarian scholars had already been destroyed or parceled up and lay beneath modern neighborhoods and businesses. Still, over the past two decades construction projects throughout greater Nashville continue to encounter ancient campsites, villages, towns, and cemeteries. Sites like Logan, where hundreds of stone box graves remained within a single 1.5-acre parcel, are probably exceptions. Nevertheless, small portions of many sites still survive. As former state archaeologist Mike Moore told us, "you always think it's the last one, until the next one."

Over the past decade Aaron's work at the Division of Archaeology has included responding to regular calls from landowners in the neighborhoods near Lipscomb University. In that area along the watershed of Brown's Creek, utility work, residential repairs, swimming pool construction, and even casual gardening continue to encounter Mississippian stone box graves that were once part of the Noel Cemetery site. Those calls have increased in frequency as original homes of the area, many of which lacked basements and occupied relatively little of their associated lots, are torn down to make way for the massive houses, large garages, and detached accessory dwelling units that make up Nashville's new residential architecture. As our city grows and changes, modern and ancient Nashville continue to encounter one another in unexpected ways.

It has been 250 years since James Robertson founded the first permanent European settlement along the Cumberland in what would become Nashville, but as the chapters in this book reveal, that period is just a tiny portion of our shared archaeological history. Nashville's deep past is an amazing collection of often-overlooked stories that include ice age animals, ancient mounds and villages, antiquarians, archaeologists, and most importantly, the cumulative legacy of more than thirteen millennia of Native American lives. Much of that past has been erased during the last century of urban and suburban growth, but so long as sites persist, there remains hope. With appreciation for and acknowledgment of the past, concerned citizens, the preservation community, developers, government organizations, and archaeologists can all work collectively, building toward Nashville's future while preserving and respecting what came before.

NASHVILLE-AREA
LEARNING OPPORTUNITIES
AND FURTHER READING

IN-PERSON OPPORTUNITIES

The *Current Research in Tennessee Archaeology* meeting is held each January in the Nashville area. This event includes presentations by professional and academic archaeologists describing recent research and investigations throughout the state. The day-long program is free and open to the general public. Information on the meeting can be found via the Tennessee Division of Archaeology's webpage.

The permanent "First Peoples" exhibit at the *Tennessee State Museum* at Bicentennial Mall State Park shares artifacts and information spanning the entirety of Native American history in Tennessee. The exhibit includes artifacts and fossils from the Nashville area, from mastodon fossils found along the Harpeth River to Mississippian salt pan artifacts unearthed during construction of the new Nashville Sounds stadium.

John Overton's historic home at Travellers Rest was built atop a Mississippian period fortified village. Today *Historic Travellers Rest* works to preserve and interpret the history of the site's first residents through exhibits and programming.

Old Stone Fort State Archaeological Park, located just outside Manchester, includes the remains of a two-thousand-year-old Woodland period earthwork overlooking the Duck River. The site has a small museum and several miles of well-maintained, attractive hiking trails. Each year the park hosts the Old Stone Fort Knap-In and Archaeoskills event, which draws flintknappers and primitive skills enthusiasts from around the region.

The Mississippian mound complex at *Mound Bottom State Archaeological Area* in Cheatham County is part of the Harpeth River State Park. The site is closed to public visitation without accompaniment by park staff or the Division of Archaeology. Both organizations offer guided tours of the site throughout the year. Information can be found on their respective social media pages or in the events listings on the Tennessee State Parks website.

The fortified Mississippian mound center at *Sellars Farm State Archaeological Area* near Lebanon in Wilson County is managed by Long Hunter State Park. There is an interpretive kiosk and 1.5-mile self-guided trail through the site that is open to the public. The Division of Archaeology also offers guided hikes at the site, which can be found on the Tennessee State Parks website.

The Nashville-based *Native History Association* conducts research and hosts a wide variety of archaeological and historical information on their webpage. The group also offers public programming and volunteer opportunities.

The *Middle Cumberland Archaeological Society* is one of the oldest continually active organizations devoted to the archaeology of Tennessee. They hold bimonthly meetings in Nashville that are open to the public and feature professional presentations on archaeological topics. Members receive the society newsletter, which includes current information on volunteer fieldwork opportunities, public programming, and museum exhibitions. You can find more information on their social media page.

The *Rutherford County Archaeological Society* hosts free programs by MTSU faculty, students, and professional archaeologists on both local and international topics. Their meeting schedule and programming information can be found on social media.

As part of the *Tennessee Archaeology Awareness Month* celebration each September, universities, parks, and organizations throughout the state host public programming. Locally, the Tennessee Council for Professional Archaeology's *Archaeology Day* celebration at Nashville's Bells Bend Park shares information on the history and archaeology of Middle Tennessee.

The Earth Experience, the Middle Tennessee Museum of Natural History in Murfreesboro is the first natural history museum in Middle Tennessee and presents an assortment of archaeological artifacts alongside interactive fossil exhibits.

FURTHER READING

The *Tennessee Division of Archaeology webpage* hosts a free digital library of sources including research reports and peer-reviewed publications. Further information on many of the sites mentioned in this volume can be found in that database. The Division of Archaeology website is also home to a digital archive of the free online journal *Tennessee Archaeology*. For those interested in reading more about the stories presented in this volume, the following list includes some accessible sources, many of which can be found via the Division of Archaeology webpage.

Antón, Mauricio. *Sabertooth*. Bloomington: Indiana University Press, 2013.

Corgan, James X., and Emmanuel Breitburg. *Tennessee's Prehistoric Vertebrates*. Tennessee Division of Geology Bulletin 84. Nashville: State of Tennessee Department of Environment and Conservation, 1996.

Jones, Joseph. *Explorations of the Aboriginal Remains of Tennessee*. Smithsonian Contributions to Knowledge 22, no. 259. Washington, DC: Smithsonian Institution, 1876.

Moore, Michael C. "Celebrating a Milestone: The Tennessee Division of Archaeology Turns 50." *Tennessee Conservationist*, Jan/Feb 2020, 12–15.

Moore, Michael C. *The Brentwood Library Site: A Mississippian Town on the Little Harpeth River, Williamson County, Tennessee*. Division of Archaeology Research Series No. 15. Nashville: Tennessee Department of Environment and Conservation, 2005.

Moore, Michael C., and Emanuel Breitburg. *Gordontown: Salvage Archaeology at a Mississippian Town in Davidson County, Tennessee*. Division of Archaeology Research Series No. 11. Nashville: Tennessee Department of Environment and Conservation, 1998.

Moore, Michael C., and Kevin E. Smith. *Archaeological Expeditions of the Peabody Museum in Middle Tennessee, 1877–1884*. Division of Archaeology Research Series No. 16. Nashville: Tennessee Department of Environment and Conservation, 2009 (revised 2016).

Myer, William E. "Two Prehistoric Villages in Middle Tennessee." *Forty-first Annual Report of the American Bureau of Ethnology to the Secretary of the Smithsonian Institution, 1919–1924*, 485–614. Washington, DC: US Government Printing Office, 1928.

Peres, Tanya M., and Aaron Deter-Wolf. *The Cumberland River Archaic of Middle Tennessee*. Gainesville: University Press of Florida, 2019.

Smith, Kevin E., and James V. Miller. *Speaking with the Ancestors: Mississippian Stone Statuary of the Tennessee-Cumberland Region.* Tuscaloosa: University of Alabama Press, 2009.

Thompson, Keith S. *The Legacy of the Mastodon: The Golden Age of Fossils in America.* New Haven, CT: Yale University Press, 2008.

NOTES

CHAPTER I

1. Keith Stuart Thomson, *The Legacy of the Mastodon: The Golden Age of Fossils in America* (New Haven, CT: Yale University Press, 2008).

2. John Haywood, *The Natural and Aboriginal History of Tennessee: Up to the First Settlements therein by the White People, in the Year 1768* (Nashville, TN: George Wilson, 1823).

3. James X. Corgan and Emanuel Breitburg, *Tennessee's Prehistoric Vertebrates*, Tennessee Division of Geology Bulletin 84 (Nashville: State of Tennessee Department of Environment and Conservation, 1996).

4. Kevin E. Smith, "The Williamson County Giant (aka A Pleistocene Mega-Human)," *Newsletter of the Middle Cumberland Archaeological Society* 38, no. 5 (2013): 2–6.

5. Park Marshall, "The Topographical Beginnings of Nashville," *Tennessee Historical Magazine* 2, no.1 (1916): 31–39.

6. Aaron Deter-Wolf and Kevin E. Smith, "Antiquarian Investigations and Archaeological Testing at the Glass Mounds Site (40WM3)," *Tennessee Archaeology* 10, no. 2 (2020): 85–108.

7. Aaron Deter-Wolf, ed., *The Fernvale Site (40WM51): A Late Archaic Occupation along the South Harpeth River in Williamson County, Tennessee*, Division of Archaeology Research Series No. 19 (Nashville: Tennessee Department of Environment and Conservation, 2013).

8. Tanya M. Peres, Teresa Ingalls, and Lacey S. Fleming, "Faunal Assemblage," in Deter-Wolf, *The Fernvale Site*, 99–114.

9. Aaron Deter-Wolf and Tanya M. Peres, "Embedded: 5,000 Years of Shell Symbolism in the Southeast," in *Trends and Traditions in Southeastern Zooar-*

chaeology, ed. Tanya M. Peres (Gainesville: University Press of Florida, 2014), 161–85.

10. Shannon Chappell Hodge and C. Brady Davis, "Bioarchaeological Analysis," in Deter-Wolf, *The Fernvale Site*, 121–58.

11. Anthony A. Volk and Jeremy A. Atkinson, "Infant and Child Death in the Human Environment of Evolutionary Adaptation," *Evolution and Human Behavior* 34, no. 3 (2013): 182–92.

12. Robert P. Mensforth, "Human Trophy Taking in Eastern North America during the Archaic Period," in *The Taking and Displaying of Human Body Parts as Trophies by Amerindians*, ed. Robert J. Chancon and David H. Dye (Boston, MA: Springer, 2017), 222–77.

13. Aaron Deter-Wolf, Tanya M. Peres, and Steven Karacic, "Ancient Native American Bone Tattooing Tools and Pigments: Evidence from Central Tennessee," *Journal of Archaeological Science: Reports* 37 (2021): 103002.

14. Kevin E. Smith, "Tennessee's Ancient Pygmy Graveyards: The 'Wonder of the Western Country,'" *Tennessee Archaeology* 7, no. 1 (2013): 42–75.

15. William E. Myer, "Two Prehistoric Villages in Middle Tennessee," *Forty-first Annual Report of the American Bureau of Ethnology to the Secretary of the Smithsonian Institution, 1919–1924* (Washington, DC: US Government Printing Office, 1928): 485–614.

16. John H. DeWitt, "William Edward Myer," *Tennessee Historical Magazine* 8, no. 4 (1925): 225–30.

17. Kevin E. Smith and Michael C. Moore, "Professional and Avocational Partnerships: Alive and Well in Middle Tennessee," *SAA Archaeological Record* 13, no. 2 (2013): 18–23.

18. Michael C. Moore, "Celebrating a Milestone: The Tennessee Division of Archaeology Turns 50," *Tennessee Conservationist*, Jan/Feb 2020, 12–15.

19. Hugh E. Berryman, "The Averbuch Skeletal Series: A Study of Biological and Social Stress at a Late Mississippian Period Site from Middle Tennessee" (PhD diss., University of Tennessee-Knoxville, 1981).

20. "Nashville Metro Area Population 1950–2020," Macrotrends LLC, accessed April 29, 2021, https://www.macrotrends.net/cities/23077/nashville/population.

21. Michael C. Moore "An Updated Review of the Tennessee State Cemetery Law and Other Statutes Regarding Prehistoric Burial Removal," *Tennessee Anthropologist* 23, no. 1&2 (1998): 55–64.

22. Michael C. Moore, *The Brentwood Library Site: A Mississippian Town on the Little Harpeth River, Williamson County, Tennessee*, Division of Archaeology Research Series No. 15 (Nashville: Tennessee Department of Environment and Conservation, 2005).

23. Kevin E. Smith and James V. Miller, *Speaking with the Ancestors: Mississippian Stone Statuary of the Tennessee-Cumberland Region* (Tuscaloosa: University of Alabama Press, 2009).

CHAPTER 2

1. "Confident Forecast: 'Road Is Up' for Nashville," *Tennessean*, January 16, 1972: 86.

2. Edward Morris, "'Wings of a Dove' Writer, Bob Ferguson, Dies at 73 in Mississippi," *CMT News*, July 23, 2001, http://www.cmt.com/news/1445337/wings-of-a-dove-writer-bob-ferguson-dies-at-73-in-mississippi.

3. John T. Dowd, "Archaeology in Middle Tennessee in the 1960s and 70s," *30 Days of Tennessee Archaeology 2014* (blog), Tennessee Council for Professional Archaeology, September 26, 2014, https://tennesseearchaeologycouncil.wordpress.com/2014/09/26/30-days-of-tennessee-archaeology-day-26-archaeology-in-middle-tennessee-in-the-1960s-and-70s.

4. Robert B. Ferguson, "The First American Site, Our Site Number: 87, Nashville Tennessee (Music City Man and the Nashville Cat)." Undated manuscript on file, Tennessee Division of Archaeology, Nashville.

5. Robert B. Ferguson, "First American Site," *SIAS Newsletter*, August 26, 1971. On file, Tennessee Division of Archaeology, Nashville.

6. John T. Dowd, "The Nashville Smilodon: An Account of the 1971 First American Center Site Investigations in Davidson County, Tennessee." *Tennessee Archaeology* 5, no. 1 (2010): 65–82.

7. John E. Guilday, "Sabertooth Cat, *Smilodon floridanus* (Leidy), and Associated Fauna from a Tennessee Cave (40DV40), the First American Site." *Journal of the Tennessee Academy of Sciences* 52, no. 3 (1977): 84–94.

8. Tom Ingram, "Dark Prehistoric Bank Cave Seems Like a Plush Ballroom," *Tennessean*, June 15, 1972, 21.

9. "Tiger in the Bank," *Time Magazine*, August 6, 1973, 53.

10. "Caves Beneath City May be Opened to General Public," *Nashville Tennessean and the Nashville American*, November 12, 1911, A4; "Nashville Caverns:

Curious and Novel Impressions of the Newly Discovered Crevice on Union Street," *Tennessean*, July 3, 1883, 4; "Wonders beneath City of Nashville: Old Citizens Relate Interesting Stories of Some Great Underground Passageways," *Nashville Tennessean and the Nashville American*, October 8, 1911, A4.

11. "Cavity under Square: Old Citizens Tell of Beatty's Cave . . ." *Nashville American*, November 9, 1902, 19.

12. "City Hall Rests on Cave: Fissures in the Solid Rock Run under Public Square," *Nashville American*, November 17, 1909, 6.

13. "Deep under the City: Mysterious Caves Far Below Nashville's Upper Stratum of Society," *Nashville American*, August 2, 1875, 5.

14. "Nashville's Labyrinths: Another Entrance to Subterranean Caverns Discovered," *Daily American*, May 24, 1876, 4.

15. *Nashville Tennessean and the Nashville American*, November 12, 1911.

16. "Cock Fights Were Staged in Cave beneath the City: Retired Engineer Says Entrance at Foot of Church Street," *Nashville Tennessean and the Nashville American*, November 15, 1911, 2.

17. "Under the City: Rambling through the Caverns of Nashville . . ." *Republican Banner*, August 15, 1874, 4.

18. "Science under Difficulties: Attempted Exploration of the Cave that Exists under Nashville," *Daily American*, April 26, 1878, 4.

19. Charles W. Wilson Jr. and Donald S. Fullerton, "Geologic Map and Mineral Resources Summary of the Nashville West Quadrangle," 1:24,000 Geologic Quadrangle Map 308 NE (Nashville: Tennessee Division of Geology, 1996).

20. *Daily American*, May 24, 1876.

21. *Nashville American*, August 2, 1897.

22. Guilday, "Sabertooth Cat, *Smilodon floridanus*."

23. Johanna L. A. Paijmans, Ross Barnett, M. Thomas P. Gilbert, M. Lisandra Zepeda-Mendoza, Jelle W. F. Reumer, John de Vos, Grant Zazula et al., "Evolutionary History of Saber-Toothed Cats Based on Ancient Mitogenomics," *Current Biology* 27, no. 21 (2017): 3330–36.

24. Mauricio Antón, *Sabertooth* (Bloomington: Indiana University Press, 2013).

25. H. Gregory McDonald, "Smilodon: A Short History of Becoming the Iconic Sabertooth," in *Smilodon: The Iconic Sabertooth*, ed. Lars H. Werdelin, H. Gregory McDonald, and Christopher A. Shaw (Baltimore, MD: Johns Hopkins University Press, 2018): 1–14.

26. H. Gregory McDonald and Lars H. Werdelin, "The Sabertooth Cat, *Smilodon populator* (Carnivora, Felidae), from Cueva del Milodón, Chile," in

Smilodon: The Iconic Sabertooth, ed. Lars H. Werdelin, H. Gregory McDonald, and Christopher A. Shaw (Baltimore, MD: Johns Hopkins University Press, 2018): 53–75.

27. Corgan and Breitburg. *Tennessee's Prehistoric Vertebrates*.

28. Stuart Fiedel, "Sudden Deaths: The Chronology of Terminal Pleistocene Megafaunal Extinction," in *American Megafaunal Extinctions at the End of the Pleistocene*, edited by Gary Haynes (New York: Springer, 2009): 21–37.

29. Larisa R. G. DeSantis, Jonathan M. Crites, Robert S. Feranec, Kena Fox-Dobbs, Aisling B. Farrell, John M. Harris, Gary T. Takeuchi, and Thure E. Cerling "Causes and Consequences of Pleistocene Megafaunal Extinctions as Revealed from Rancho La Brea Mammals," *Current Biology* 29 (2019): 2488–95.

30. Larisa R. G. DeSantis, Blaine W. Schubert, Jessica R. Scott, and Peter S. Ungar, "Implications of Diet for the Extinction of Saber-Toothed Cats and American Lions," *PLoS ONE* 7, no. 12 (2012): e52453.

31. Larisa R. G. DeSantis, "Dietary Ecology of Smilodon." In *Smilodon: The Iconic Sabertooth*, ed. Lars H. Werdelin, H. Gregory McDonald, and Christopher A. Shaw (Baltimore, MD: Johns Hopkins University Press, 2018): 153–70.

32. Geordie L. Duckler and Blaire Van Valkenburgh, "Exploring the Health of Late Pleistocene Mammals: The Use of Harris Lines," *Journal of Vertebrate Paleontology* 18, no. 1 (1996): 180–88.

33. Blaire Van Valkenburgh and Fritz Hertel, "Tough Times at La Brea: Tooth Breakage in Large Carnivores of the Late Pleistocene, *Science* 261, no. 5120 (1993): 456–59.

34. DeSantis, Schubert, Scott, and Ungar, "Implications of Diet."

35. Dowd, "The Nashville Smilodon."

36. Jeff Legwold, "Logo a Saber-toothed Tiger: Fans to Vote on Nickname," *Tennessean*, September 25, 1997, 1C.

37. Aaron Deter-Wolf, "The First American Cave Site Revisited," *Courier* 47, no. 2 (2009): 4–5.

38. Brooks Batten, "Bones from Nashville Predators Origin Come Home," *Predators News*, NHL.com, November 11, 2016, https://www.nhl.com/predators/news/bones-of-nashville-predators-origin-come-to-bridgestone-arena/c-283640230.

CHAPTER 3

1. Ted Goebel, Heather L. Smith, Lyndsay DiPietro, Michael R. Waters, Bryan Hockett, Kelly E. Graf, Robert Gal et al., "Serpentine Hot Springs, Alaska: Results of Excavations and Implications for the Age and Significance of Northern Fluted Points," *Journal of Archaeological Science* 40, no. 12 (2013): 4222–33.

2. Jeremy L. Green, Gina M. Semprebon, and Nikos Solounias, "Reconstructing the Palaeodiet of Florida *Mammut americanum* via Low-magnification Stereomicroscopy," *Palaeogeography, Palaeoclimatology, Palaeoecology* 223, no. 1–2 (2005): 34–48; Chelsea L. Teale and Norton G. Miller. "Mastodon Herbivory in Mid-latitude Late-Pleistocene Boreal Forests of Eastern North America," *Quaternary Research* 78, no. 1 (2012): 72–81.

3. Thomson, *The Legacy of the Mastodon.*

4. Tennessee Division of Archaeology, State Site File Records. Nashville, Tennessee.

5. Corgan, and Breitburg, *Tennessee's Prehistoric Vertebrates.*

6. Ellen V. Piers, "Girard Troost Pioneer Scientist," *Peabody Journal of Education* 30, no. 5 (1953): 265–74.

7. Rachel Stephens, "Curious Men and Their Curiosities: Ralph E. W. Earl's Nashville Museum and the Precedent of Charles Willson Peale," *Early American Studies: An Interdisciplinary Journal* 16, no. 3 (2018): 545–77.

8. Gerard Troost, "On the Localities in Tennessee in which Bones of the Gigantic Mastodon and *Megalonyx Jeffersonii* Are Found," *Transactions of the Geological Society of Pennsylvania*, Vol 1 and 2 (1835): 139–46, 236–43.

9. Gerard Troost, "The Great Mastodon: Improperly Called 'Mammoth,' Found in the Vicinity of Nashville," *Literary Journal, and Weekly Register of Science and the Arts* 1, no. 30 (1834): 234.

10. "A MASTODON: A Relic of the Ages Discovered by Workmen: A Mammoth Tusk Unearthed Near Murphy's Sulphur Well," *Daily American*, July 21, 1887, 5.

11. Emanuel Breitburg and John B. Broster. "A Hunt for Big Game: Does Coats-Hines Site Confirm Human/Mastodon Contact?" *Tennessee Conservationist* 61, no. 4 (1995): 18–26.

12. Emanuel Breitburg, John B. Broster, Arthur L. Reesman, and Richard G. Stearns, "The Coats-Hines Site: Tennessee's First Paleoindian-Mastodon Association." *Current Research in the Pleistocene* 13 (1996): 6–8.

13. Breitburg and Broster, "A Hunt for Big Game"

14. Kaitlyn A. Thomas, Brett A. Story, Metin I. Eren, Briggs Buchanan, Brian N. Andrews, Michael J. O'Brien, and David J. Meltzer, "Explaining the Origin of Fluting in North American Pleistocene Weaponry," *Journal of Archaeological Science* 81 (2017): 23–30.

15. J. Víctor Moreno-Mayar, Ben A. Potter, Lasse Vinner, Matthias Steinrücken, Simon Rasmussen, Jonathan Terhorst, John A. Kamm et al., "Terminal Pleistocene Alaskan Genome Reveals First Founding Population of Native Americans," *Nature* 553 (2018): 203–7.

16. Rémy Crassard, Vincent Charpentier, Joy McCorriston, Jérémie Vosges, Sofiane Bouzid, and Michael D. Petraglia, "Fluted-point Technology in Neolithic Arabia: An Independent Invention Far from the Americas," *PLoS ONE* 15, no. 8 (2020): e0236314.

17. David G. Anderson, D. Shane Miller, Stephen J. Yerka, J. Christopher Gillam, Erik N. Johanson, Derek T. Anderson, Albert C. Goodyear, and Ashley M. Smallwood, "PIDBA (Paleoindian Database of the Americas) 2010: Current Status and Findings," *Archaeology of Eastern North America* 38 (2010): 63–90.

18. John B. Broster, Mark R. Norton, D. Shane Miller, Jesse W. Tune, and Jon D. Baker, "Tennessee's Paleoindian Record," in *In the Eastern Fluted Point Tradition*, vol. 1, ed. Joseph A. M. Guengrich (Salt Lake City: University of Utah Press, 2013): 299–314.

19. Lisa Nagaoka, Torben Rick, and Steve Wolverton, "The Overkill Model and Its Impact on Environmental Research," *Ecology and Evolution* 8, no. 19 (2018): 1–14.

20. Donald K. Grayson and David J. Meltzer, "Revisiting Paleoindian Exploitation of Extinct North American Mammals," *Journal of Archaeological Science* 56 (2015): 177–93.

21. David J. Meltzer, "Pleistocene Overkill and North American Mammalian Extinctions." *Annual Review of Anthropology* 44, no. 1 (2015): 33–53.

22. Aaron Deter-Wolf, Jesse W. Tune, and John B. Broster. "Excavations and Dating of Late Pleistocene and Paleoindian Deposits at the Coats-Hines Site," *Tennessee Archaeology* 5, no. 2 (2011): 142–56.

23. Tennessee Department of Education, Standard 5.27, Tennessee Social Studies Standards, 2018, https://www.tn.gov/content/dam/tn/education/standards/ss/Social_Studies_Standards.pdf.

24. Jesse W. Tune, Michael R. Waters, Kayla A. Schmalle, Larisa R. G. DeSantis, and George D. Kamenov, "Assessing the Proposed Pre-last Glacial Maximum Human Occupation of North America at Coats-Hines-Litchy, Tennessee, and Other Sites," *Quaternary Science Reviews* 186 (2018): 47–59.

25. Jesse W. Tune, "Settling into the Younger Dryas: Human Behavioral Adaptations during the Pleistocene to Holocene Transition in the Midsouth United States" (PhD diss., Texas A&M University, 2015).

26. Breitburg, Broster, Reesman, and Stearns, "The Coats-Hines Site: Tennessee's First Paleoindian-Mastodon Association."

27. Michael B. Collins, "Discerning Clovis Subsistence from Stone Artifacts and Site Distributions on the Southern Plains Periphery," in *Foragers of the Terminal Pleistocene in North America*, ed. Renee B. Walker and Boyce N. Driskell (Lincoln: University of Nebraska Press, 2007), 59–87; Ashley K. Lemke and Cinda Timperley, "Preliminary Analysis of Turtle Material from the Gault Site, Texas," *Current Research in the Pleistocene* 25 (2018): 115–18; Steven R. Kuehn, "Late Paleoindian Subsistence Strategies in the Western Great Lakes Region Evidence for Generalized Foraging from Northern Wisconsin," in *Foragers of the Terminal Pleistocene in North America*, ed. Renee B. Walker and Boyce N. Driskell., (Lincoln: University of Nebraska Press, 2007), 88–98.

28. Stephen B. Carmody, Kandace D. Hollenbach, and Elic M. Weitzel, "Prehistoric Foodways from the Dust Cave Site," in *Baking, Bourbon, and Black Drink: Foodways Archaeology in the American Southeast*, ed. Tanya M. Peres and Aaron Deter-Wolf (Tuscaloosa: University of Alabama Press, 2018): 102–18.

29. Renee B. Walker, "Hunting in the Late Paleoindian Period: Faunal Remains from Dust Cave, Alabama," in *Foragers of the Terminal Pleistocene in North America*, ed. Renee B. Walker and Boyce N. Driskell (Lincoln: University of Nebraska Press, 2007): 99–115.

CHAPTER 4

1. Aaron Deter-Wolf and Leslie Straub, "Archaic Shell-Bearing Site Investigations in the Middle Cumberland River Valley," in *The Cumberland River Archaic of Middle Tennessee*, ed. Tanya M. Peres and Aaron Deter-Wolf (Gainesville: University Press of Florida, 2019): 15–41.

2. Tanya M. Peres and Aaron Deter-Wolf, introduction to *The Cumberland River Archaic of Middle Tennessee*, ed. Tanya M. Peres and Aaron Deter-Wolf (Gainesville: University Press of Florida, 2019): 1–14.

3. Tanya M. Peres and Aaron Deter-Wolf, *The Cumberland River Archaic of Middle Tennessee* (Gainesville: University Press of Florida, 2019).

4. Hazel R. Delcourt, "Late Quaternary Vegetation History of the Eastern Highland Rim and Adjacent Cumberland Plateau of Tennessee," *Ecological Monographs* 49, no. 3 (1979): 255–80.

5. Andrew Gillreath-Brown and Aaron Deter-Wolf, "Modeling Archaic Settlement Patterns and Ecology in the Middle Cumberland River Valley of Tennessee," in *The Cumberland River Archaic of Middle Tennessee*, ed. Tanya M. Peres and Aaron Deter-Wolf (Gainesville: University Press of Florida, 2019): 145–66.

6. David G. Anderson, "Archaic Mounds and the Archaeology of Southeastern Tribal Societies," in *Signs of Power: The Development of Complexity in the Southeast*, ed. Jon L. Gibson and Philip J. Carr (Tuscaloosa: University of Alabama Press, 2003): 270–99; Cheryl Claassen, *Feasting with Shellfish in the Southern Ohio Valley: Archaic Sacred Sites and Rituals* (Knoxville: University of Tennessee Press, 2010).

7. Aaron Deter-Wolf, "The Ensworth School Site (40DV184): A Middle Archaic Benton Occupation along the Harpeth River Drainage in Middle Tennessee," *Tennessee Archaeology* 1, no. 1 (2004): 18–35; Aaron Deter-Wolf and Tanya M. Peres, "Embedded: 5,000 Years of Shell Symbolism in the Southeast," in *Trends and Traditions in Southeastern Zooarchaeology*, ed. Tanya M. Peres (Gainesville: University Press of Florida, 2014): 161–85; Tanya M. Peres, Aaron Deter-Wolf, Joey Keasler, and Shannon Chappell Hodge, "Faunal Remains from an Archaic Period Cave in the Southeastern United States," *Journal of Archaeological Science: Reports* 8 (2016): 187–99; Deter-Wolf, Peres, and Karacic, "Ancient Native American Bone Tattooing Tools and Pigments."

8. Jesse W. Tune, "The Paleoindian and Early Archaic Record in Tennessee: A Review of the Tennessee Fluted Point Survey," *Tennessee Archaeology* 8, no. 1-2 (Summer 2016): 24–41.

9. "RAPID: Emergency Shoreline Assessment and Sampling of Archaeological Sites along the Cumberland River in Middle Tennessee," National Science Foundation Federal Award ID No. 1048351, https://www.nsf.gov/awardsearch/showAward?AWD_ID=1048351.

10. Tanya M. Peres and Aaron Deter-Wolf, "The 2010 Cumberland River Survey Emergency Survey and Archaic Shell Site Composition in the Western Middle Cumberland River Valley," in *The Cumberland River Archaic of Middle Tennessee*, ed. Tanya M. Peres and Aaron Deter-Wolf (Gainesville: University Press of Florida, 2019): 45–55.

11. Tanya M. Peres, Aaron Deter-Wolf, Kelly L. Ledford, Joey Keasler, Ryan W. Robinson, and Andrew R. Wyatt, "Archaeological Investigations at 40DV7," in *The Cumberland River Archaic of Middle Tennessee*, ed. Tanya M. Peres and Aaron Deter-Wolf (Gainesville: University Press of Florida, 2019): 56–74.

12. Robert T. Dillon Jr., *The Ecology of Freshwater Molluscs* (Cambridge, UK: Cambridge University Press, 2000).

13. Lynn B. Starnes and Arthur E. Bogan, "The Mussels (Mollusca: Bivalvia: Unionidae) of Tennessee," *American Malacological Bulletin* 6, no. 1 (1988): 19–37.

14. Thomas M. N. Lewis and Madeline Kneberg Lewis, *Eva: An Archaic Site* (Knoxville: University of Tennessee Press, 1960).

15. Patrick Baker, "Issues in Marine Fisheries and Conservation," in *The Mollusks: A Guide to Their Study, Collection, and Preservation*, ed. Charles F. Sturm, Timothy A. Pierce, and Ángel Valdés (Boca Raton, FL: Universal Publishers, 2006): 381–416.

16. Cheryl Claassen, "Analytical Study of Shellfish from the DeWeese Mound, Kentucky," in *Archaeology of the Middle Green River Region, Kentucky*, ed. William H. Marquardt and Patty Jo Watson (Gainesville: Florida Museum of Natural History, University of Florida, 2005): 279–94.

17. Tanya M. Peres and Aaron Deter-Wolf, "The Shell-Bearing Archaic in the Middle Cumberland River Valley," *Southeastern Archaeology* 35, no. 3 (2016): 237–50.

18. Peres, Deter-Wolf, Ledford, Keasler, Robinson, and Wyatt, "Archaeological Investigations at 40DV7," 74.

19. Aaron Deter-Wolf and Jesse W. Tune, "Ceramic Analysis," in *The Fernvale Site (40WM51): A Late Archaic Occupation along the South Harpeth River in Williamson County, Tennessee*, ed. Aaron Deter-Wolf, Division of Archaeology Research Series No. 19. (Nashville: Tennessee Department of Environment and Conservation, 2013), 19–28.

20. Walter E. Klippel and Darcy F. Morey, "Contextual and Nutritional Analysis of Freshwater Gastropods from Middle Archaic Deposits at the Hayes Site, Middle Tennessee," *American Antiquity* 51, no. 4 (1986): 799–813.

21. Mary L. Simon, "A Regional and Chronological Synthesis of Archaic Period Plant Use in the Midcontinent," in *Archaic Societies: Diversity and Complexity across the Midcontinent*, ed. Thomas E. Emerson, Dale L. McElrath, and Andrew C. Fortier (Albany: State University of New York Press, 2009): 81–114.

22. Tanya M. Peres and Aaron Deter-Wolf, "A New View of the Shell-Bearing Archaic in the Middle Cumberland River Valley," in *The Cumberland River Archaic of Middle Tennessee*, ed. Tanya M. Peres and Aaron Deter-Wolf (Gainesville: University Press of Florida, 2019): 167–84.

CHAPTER 5

1. Margaret Renkl, "A Monument the Old South Would Like to Ignore," *New York Times*, January 29, 2018, http://www.nytimes.com/2018/01/29/opinion/south-monuments-nashville.html.

2. Virgil R. Beasley III, Charles Van de Kree, Ted Karpynec, Meghan Weaver, Travis Real, Cassandra Medeiros, Elinor Crook, and Cristina I. Oliveira, *Historical Background Research and a Ground Penetrating Radar Survey Associated with the Greer Stadium Redevelopment Project in Nashville, Davidson County, Tennessee.* Huntsville: Tennessee Valley Archaeological Research, 2018, http://www.nashville.gov/Portals/0/SiteContent/MayorsOffice/docs/news/TVAR%20Greer%20Stadium%20Report.pdf.

3. Joseph Jones, "Explorations of the Aboriginal Remains of Tennessee," *Smithsonian Contributions to Knowledge* 22, no. 259 (1876): 1–171.

4. Gerard Troost, "An Account of Some Ancient Indian Remains in Tennessee," *Transactions of the American Ethnological Society* 1 (1845): 355–65.

5. John Haywood, *The Natural and Aboriginal History of Tennessee: Up to the First Settlements therein by the White People, in the Year 1768* (Nashville, TN: George Wilson, 1823).

6. Richard L. Forstall, *Population of States and Counties of the United States: 1790–1990*, Department of Commerce, US Bureau of the Census (Washington DC: US Government Printing Bureau, 1996).

7. Andrew Jackson, "Second Annual Message, December 6, 1830," *A Compilation of the Messages and Papers of the Presidents*, ed. James D. Richardson, vol. 3. (New York: Bureau of National Literature, 1897), 1062–92.

8. Phillip Hodge, "Partners in Preservation: The Rediscovery of the First Bridge over the Cumberland River," *30 Days of Tennessee Archaeology 2015* (blog), Tennessee Council for Professional Archaeology, Sep-

tember 10, 2015, https://tennesseearchaeologycouncil.wordpress.
com/2015/09/10/30-days-of-tennessee-archaeology-2015-day-10.

9. Betsy Phillips, "The Old Whites Creek Road, the Trail of Tears, and
the First East Nashville," *Nashville Scene*, January 31, 2017, https://www.
nashvillescene.com/news/pith-in-the-wind/article/20850581/the-old-
whites-creek-road-the-trail-of-tears-and-the-first-east-nashville.

10. Gates P. Thruston, *Antiquities of Tennessee and the Adjacent States and the
State of Aboriginal Society in the Scale of Civilization Represented by Them*
(Cincinnati, OH: Robert Clarke & Co, 1890).

11. Robert B. Ferguson, *The Middle Cumberland Culture*, Vanderbilt University
Publications in Anthropology No. 3 (Nashville, TN: Vanderbilt University,
Department of Anthropology, 1972).

12. Kevin E. Smith, "The Middle Cumberland Region: Mississippian Archaeology in North Central Tennessee," (PhD diss., Vanderbilt University, 1992.)

13. Moore, *The Brentwood Library Site*.

14. *Nashville American*, "Dr. W. H. Jarman Passes Away after Long Illness," July
6, 1904, 6.

15. Michael C. Moore and Kevin E. Smith, *Archaeological Expeditions of the
Peabody Museum in Middle Tennessee, 1877–1884*, Division of Archaeology
Research Series No. 16 (Nashville: Tennessee Department of Environment
and Conservation, 2009).

16. Michael C. Moore, Kevin E. Smith, and Stephen T. Rogers, "Middle Tennessee Archeology and the Enigma of the George Woods." *Tennessee Historical Quarterly* 69, no. 4 (2010): 320–29.

17. Frederic W. Putnam, "The Stone Graves of Brentwood, Tennessee," *Kan-
sas City Review of Science* 6, no. 9-10 (1883): 526–29.

18. Kevin E. Smith and Michael C. Moore, "Middle Cumberland Mississippian
Archaeology: Past, Present, and Future Directions," *Tennessee Archaeology*
9, no. 2 (2018): 170–200.

19. Moore and Smith, *Archaeological Expeditions of the Peabody Museum*.

20. Aaron Deter-Wolf, Sunny Fleming, and Sarah Levithol Eckhardt. "Return
to the Great Mound Group: 2016 Investigations at Mound Bottom State
Archaeological Area," *Tennessee Archaeology* 9, no. 2 (2016): 103–16.

21. Michael C. Moore, David H. Dye, and Kevin E. Smith, "WPA Excavations
at the Mound Bottom and Pack Sites in Middle Tennessee, 1936–1940," in
New Deal Archaeology in Tennessee: Intellectual, Methodological, and Theoret-

ical Contributions, ed. David H. Dye (Tuscaloosa: University of Alabama Press, 2016): 116–37.

22. Robert V. Sharp, Kevin E. Smith, and David H. Dye, "Cahokians and the Circulation of Ritual Goods in the Middle Cumberland Region," in *Cahokia in Context: Hegemony and Diaspora*, ed. Charles H. McNutt and Ryan M. Parish (Gainesville: University of Florida Press, 2020): 319–51.

23. Bryan Wener, "Re-Envisioning Greater Cahokia" (ArcGIS Story Map), Illinois State Archaeological Survey," University of Illinois Urbana-Champaign, 2012, https://www.arcgis.com/apps/Cascade/index.html?appid=a58c2043100d4f3a891dc83d9bc00c2e.

24. Justin Jennings, *Globalizations and the Ancient World* (Cambridge, UK: Cambridge University Press, 2011).

25. Dorian J. Burnette, David H. Dye, and Arleen A. Hill, "Drought, Disruption, and Deities: Late Prehistoric Environmental Change in Tennessee" (paper presented at the Current Research in Tennessee Archaeology 30th Annual Meeting, Burns, TN, Jan. 26–27, 2018).

26. Edward R. Cook, Richard R. Heim Jr., Celine Herweijer, and Connie Woodhouse, "Megadroughts in North America: Placing IPCC Projections of Hydroclimatic Change in a Long-Term Palaeoclimate Context," *Journal of Quaternary Science* 25 (2010): 48–61.

27. Wayne C. Palmer, *Meteorological Drought*, Research Paper No. 45 (Washington DC: US Dept. of Commerce, Weather Bureau, 1965).

28. Scott C. Meeks and David G. Anderson, "Drought, Subsistence Stress, and Population Dynamics: Assessing Mississippian Abandonment of the Vacant Quarter," in *Soils, Climate and Society: Archaeological Investigations in Ancient America*, ed. John D. Wingard and Sue Eileen Hayes (Boulder: University Press of Colorado, 2013): 61–84.

29. Heather Worne, "Conflicting Spaces: Bioarchaeological and Geophysical Perspectives on Warfare in the Middle Cumberland Region of Tennessee," (PhD diss., Binghamton, University, 2011).

30. Christina L. Fojas, "Modeling Prehistoric Health in the Middle Cumberland Region of Tennessee: Mississippian Populations on the Threshold of Collapse" (PhD diss., University of Tennessee-Knoxville, 2016).

31. Berryman, "The Averbuch Skeletal Series."

32. Emanuel Breitburg and Michael C. Moore, "Mortuary Analysis," in *The Brentwood Library Site: A Mississippian Town on the Little Harpeth River, Wil-*

liamson County, Tennessee, ed. Michael C. Moore, Division of Archaeology Research Series No. 15 (Nashville: Tennessee Department of Environment and Conservation, 2015), 123–42.

33. Anthony N. Krus and Charles R. Cobb, "The Mississippian Fin-de-Siècle in the Middle Cumberland Region of Tennessee," *American Antiquity* 83, no. 2 (2018): 302–19.

34. David H. Dye, "The Great Serpent Cult in the MidSouth" (paper presented at the Current Research in Tennessee Archaeology 21st Annual Meeting, Nashville, TN, Jan. 30–31, 2009); Scott C. Meeks, Jacob Lulewicz, Shawn Patch, Kevin E. Smith, and Lynne R. Sullivan, "Middle Cumberland to Dallas: Constructing Peace in the Valley" (paper presented at the 84th Annual Meeting of the Society for American Archaeology, Albuquerque, NM, April 10–14, 2019).

35. Broxton W. Bird, Jeremy J. Wilson, William P. Gilhooly III, Byron A. Steinman, and Lucas Stamps, "Midcontinental Native American Population Dynamics and Late Holocene Hydroclimate Extremes," *Scientific Reports* 7 (2017): article no. 41628; A. J. White, Lora R. Stevens, Varenka Lorenzi, Samuel E. Munoz, Sissel Schroeder, Angelica Cao, and Taylor Bogdanovich, "Fecal Stanols Show Simultaneous Flooding and Seasonal Precipitation Change Correlate with Cahokia's Population Decline," *PNAS* 116, no. 12 (2019): 5461–66.

36. David C. Lund, Jean Lynch-Stieglitz, and William B. Curry, "Gulf Stream Density Structure and Transport during the Past Millennium," *Nature* 444, no. 7119 (2006): 601–4.

37. Stephen Williams, "The Vacant Quarter and Other Late Events in the Lower Valley," in *Towns and Temples along the Mississippi*, ed. David H. Dye and Cheryl Ann Cox (Tuscaloosa: University of Alabama Press, 1990): 170–80.

ABOUT THE AUTHORS

AARON DETER-WOLF is a prehistoric archaeologist for the Tennessee Division of Archaeology. TANYA M. PERES is an associate professor in the Department of Anthropology at Florida State University. Since 2007 they have collaborated on excavations and analyses of archaeological sites throughout Middle Tennessee. Their research includes studies of animal use and symbolism, ritual complexity in forager societies of the Cumberland River watershed, and foodways archaeology. Together they are the editors of *The Cumberland River Archaic of Middle Tennessee* and *Baking, Bourbon, and Black Drink: Foodways Archaeology in the American Southeast.*

9 780826 502155